THE TROJAN HORSE PRESIDENT

OBSERVATIONS AND OPINIONS ABOUT BARACK OBAMA'S LEADERSHIP, PERSONALITY, AND POLITICS

Peter A. Olsson and Laurence F. Messner

Strategic Book Publishing and Rights Co.

Strategic Book Publishing and Rights Co., LLC
USA | Singapore
www.sbpra.com

For information about special discounts for bulk purchases, please contact Strategic Book Publishing and Rights Co., LLC. Special Sales, at bookorder@sbpra.net.

ISBN: 978-1-950015-13-9

Introduction

Barack Obama and his "Hope and Change" for America presented a political Trojan Horse phenomenon. Obama, through clever political manipulation, presidential dictates, and speech-making brought a liberal, progressivist, socialistic political vision to America. Obama has used sophisticated Saul Alinsky political tactics to construct his Trojan Horse in America. He has tried to change America from within by distorting our political system. Obama has tried to seduce Americans with a utopian, idealized, romantic, globalized, political vision of America. According to Obama, we are not an exceptional country. We are, in Obama's mind, merely another tribe in his vision of where the best history of the collective human village is going.

Both authors had high hopes when Barack Obama was elected the first mulatto president of America. We were impressed with Obama's gift for moving and eloquent speeches. As both black and white himself, Obama had a unique opportunity. We had hopes that Obama would bring black America and white America together to continue our country's solid progress toward freedom and justice for all.

After a severe economic crisis, we hoped for the return of American economic prosperity, military power, and spiritual leadership for peace in the world through American strength of leadership.

We have been sorely disappointed in Mr. Obama!

We soon became concerned about Obama's leadership and personality perturbations. Obama's defective leadership and personality disorder had /has implications for our country's safety, constitutional integrity, and stability.

As a retired psychiatrist and psychoanalyst, Dr. Olsson experienced accumulating intuitions about the way Obama's verbal and non-verbal behavior fit patterns typical of a form of narcissistic personality disorder called the "AS- If" pattern. As time has gone on, the pattern has taken on malignant dimensions.

Lieutenant Colonel Messner is a retired military leader and college professor specializing in the teaching of leadership. Messner has concluded that Obama's leadership style is ineffective to the point of being dangerous to America. The fabric of emperor Obama's new clothes has been so cleverly created that it took years before the malignant nature of it has become apparent to more and more observers. The Trojan Horse, Chameleon, and radical in moderate clothing seem apt metaphors about Mr. Obama. Obama's political Trojan Horse is, at its core, a sophisticated neo-Marxist amalgam of socialism and creative use of Obama's brand of "social justice" propaganda vaunted as America's true values.

Many dimensions of Obama's incompetent leadership and indecisive, unstable personality is found in what he doesn't say and do. Extensive dithering about key decisions on Obama's part have appeared to some as careful pondering. It has taken years to see the negative results of Obama's narcissistic style of decision-making.

Surprisingly, Obama won re-election because of Mr. Romney's passive, too gentlemanly campaign against Obama. A key moment occurred when a liberal media moderator in a presidential debate (Candy Crowley) abandoned her neutral role to protect and answer for Obama about the Benghazi terror attack. Romney passively backed-off rather than confronting Ms. Crowley about her inappropriateness and pursuing Obama further about his role during the Benghazi tragedy and other key issues. Obama both seduced and was pampered and protected by the American mainstream media which suspended vigorous investigative reporting about his development as a person, his mentors, and the narrative he created and in which he cloaked himself.

This book is a stark and serious polemic. It is presented in the form of an ongoing exchange of informal e-mails, letters, discussions and didactic essays. It is presented here as they were originally written and may contain errors of spelling, grammar and syntax as they were written with sincerity and, sometimes, passion and were not edited at the time. Our unvarnished observations, speculations, criticisms and conclusions about Mr. Obama reflect our emerging and steady disillusionment, dismay about, and eventual thorough dislike of Mr. Obama. We have no apologies about our conclusions about Obama, his leadership and personality pattern. We hope that our observations will help prevent the damaging implications for America of his legacy and post-presidency when he becomes a progressivist celebrity community-disorganizer- in- chief. Possibly a world- organizer-in-chief.

Further, Dr. Olsson's observations and opinions about Obama's personality patterns and behavior are based on reading Mr. Obama's books about himself, his verbal and non-verbal communications at his speeches and public appearances and not on a professional diagnosis obtained during interviews and examinations of Mr. Obama.

The following articles, opinions, discussions and correspondence all took place from soon after Barack Hussein Obama's election to the Presidency of the United States of America until just before the presidential election of 2016.

THE CORRESPONDENCE:
Two Professors' Notes and Exchanges About Barack Obama's Personality, Leadership and Political Decision-Making.

BARACK OBAMA'S FATHER SUBSTITUTES

In our opinion, Frank Marshal Davis (A Marxist) was a huge influence on Barack Obama when he was in High School in Hawaii. Probably more than Barrack Obama senior, whose Socialism was more at a distance (See---East Africa Journal, July 1965. Pp 26-32. "Problems Facing Our Socialism" by Barak H. Obama. Barak senior makes some astute observations about Kenyan economic issues of the time but Obama's father is very critical of free enterprise and sees no "theoretical problem with 100% taxes if it helps citizens' needs.")

Rev. Jeremiah Wright Jr. was Mr. Obama's pastor and even baptized Obama's children. We believe that Wright's "Black Liberation Theology" very likely had a strong influence on young man Obama. Obama did renounce Wright's inflammatory racist statements during Obama's campaign for president. Obama claimed never to have heard his pastor's racist rants. Selective hearing is a good protection for a would-be politician.

In addition, we believe that Saul Alinsky was an intellectual mentor regarding community organizing ideas that Obama taught to groups of "organizers" in Chicago. One can observe Obama constantly using applications of Saul Alinsky's "Rules for Radicals" in his political tactics. In fact, Obama is a past master of these cynical but powerful political tactics.

The reader can apply his or her thinking toward Barack Obama's use of Saul Alinsky's political strategies, tactics and actions. Barack Obama rides a Trojan Horse using an Alinsky saddle. An article from Wikipedia ***Rules for Radicals: A Pragmatic Primer for Realistic Radicals*** (https://en.wikipedia.org/wiki/Rules_for_Radicals) refers to a 1971 book by community activist and writer Saul D. Alinsky about how to successfully run a movement for change. It was the last book that Alinsky wrote and was published shortly before his death in 1972. His goal for the *Rules for Radicals* was to create a guide for future community organizers, to use in uniting low-income communities, or "Have-Nots", in order for them to gain social, political, legal, and economic power.

We select five of Alinsky's "rules" as examples of how Obama makes use of them.

* RULE 1: "Power is not only what you have, but what the enemy thinks you have. Power is derived from two main sources – money and people. 'Have-Nots' must build power from flesh and blood." Obama seeks to claim identity as a black American championing the underclass of America. Actually, he comes from a black Kenyan father and a white Midwest, American mother who, along with his grandparents, oversaw his rearing in several atypical middle-class settings.

* RULE 3: "Whenever possible, go outside the expertise of the enemy. Look for ways to increase insecurity, anxiety and uncertainty." Obama did this constantly about his healthcare plan in efforts to frighten Americans about the stability of their healthcare. He falsely promised that they could best keep their healthcare and their doctors under his plan.

* RULE 5: "Ridicule is man's most potent weapon. There is no defense. It's irrational. It's infuriating." George Bush and Republicans were Obama's frequent target for ridicule about the economy and policy issues.

* RULE 10: "If you push a negative hard enough, it will push through and become a positive. Violence from the other side can win the public to your side because the public sympathizes with the underdog. Unions in the early to mid-20th Century incurred management's wrath, often in the form of violence that eventually brought public sympathy to their side." Obama and his biased Attorney General Eric Holder made use of subtle innuendo to convey to the black community in America that law enforcement officers were biased in cruel ways toward black Americans.

For example, in August 2014 a false narrative about the killing of Michael Brown was not disputed by either Obama or Holder even though they knew that the "Hands up. Don't shoot" expression was a lie and has even continued as a movement and protest against police.

* RULE 12: "Pick the target, freeze it, personalize it, and polarize it. Cut off the support network and isolate the target from sympathy. Go after people and not institutions; people hurt faster than institutions. This is cruel, but very effective. Direct, personalized criticism and ridicule works." This rule was illustrated when Obama personally invited Republican Congressman and expert on healthcare finances, Paul Ryan, as a special bipartisan guest to Georgetown University. This gathering was to address Obama's healthcare speech but was used to belittle and mock Ryan and his ideas. On another occasion, Obama even shamed and blamed the U. S. Supreme Court Justices at his 2010 State of the Union address! The reader can read Alinsky and make many further observations about Obama's political tactics.

OBAMA'S NESTS OF LIES*, INEPTITUDE and IMPULSIVIVENESS

*Lies can be things said and done, or as a corollary, things not done, or not said.

Peter Olsson

(1) Obama Care—Far beyond the website debacle—"You can keep your doctor?" (If you can find her), "you can keep your insurance plan if you like it?" (If it still exists?) "Costs of medical care will come down. (really?")

(2) Benghazi Bloodgate—It was due to a video? The Egyptian Arab spring was hopeful? We didn't have time or resources to save our ambassador et.al.? Blood is on the hands of Obama (BHO) and Secretary of State Hillary Clinton who played political cover up at the highest level.

(3) IRS---The most far reaching lie, nest scandal. It didn't take a direct order from Obama to do the anti -Tea Party, anti-conservative deeds, just a core of politically ambitious Obama minions (Lois Lerner is an example!).

(4) Syria---the red herring rescue lie for BHO was/is that he took some noble stand about gas attacks in Syria as if his cowardly compromise with Putin solved the dilemma of over a hundred thousand innocents killed by Assad. BHO has helped Putin retain power and prestige. Obama also said "Assad must go and yet he hasn't, and Obama blinked as his redline about chemical attacks on Assad's political opponents turned bright yellow. Our powerful Navy and Air Force stood idly by as the liberal media helped foist upon America's Obama's supposed sagacious ponderings resulting in avoidance of war.

(5) Egypt---Arab Spring sprung and was undone by Obama's supporting the Radical Fascist Muslim Brotherhood (MB). Obama even had suspected MB sympathizers in his administration!

(6) Afghanistan--- BHO and his "Rules of Engagement" have led to many deaths of our soldiers in combat there. They can't even shoot bad guys till they are fired upon! Afghanistan Commander, General Stanley McChrystal, had Obama pegged for the dithering passivism that Obama projects. These were described in detail in the Rolling Stone article, "The Runaway General: The Profile that Brought Down McChrystal by Michael Hastings on June 22, 2010.

(7) Iraq---No Status of Forces Agreement was insisted upon by Obama or Obamists. A fragile victory in Iraq turns into a loss via Obama's ordered premature departure.

(8) Iran---The absurd contention that relaxed sanctions are a good carrot to get diplomacy going with Iran and that sanctions can easily be returned if/when Iran cheats, according to BHO. That is wishful thinking as Snap-back of sanctions would never work. In addition the bogus deal with Iran was spiced up with a plane load of cash.

(9) After a year+ of Obama-Ville there is "Trouble in River City".

We have a list of instances of Obama's premature, cocky, and impulsive comments and actions/inactions. Obama holds himself out as a pragmatic, thoughtful and careful decision-maker. He lectures us with finger-points, scolding and teleprompter shaming; and, Bush-blaming performances, but it is at impromptu moments that he has premature ejaculation of the mouth. As worrisome as Obama's impulsive verbiage is at times, his lack of action at other times is as worrisome. Like most people with personality disorders, Obama seems to not learn from his mistakes. **He seemingly can't resist cocky, provocative, opponent- baiting Alinskyesque comments that play to his leftwing base.** **

**THE LIST

1---   Obama impulsively says the U.S. Army base at Guantanamo, Cuba (GITMO) will be closed in a year, but after he starts studying it, he realizes it shouldn't be closed and it's still open, with no clear sensible reason to close it

2---   Obama says at a press conference that we need to carefully investigate the allegations of his friend and hot-headed Harvard Professor Gates' charges of misconduct by a Cambridge Mass policeman, but in the same impulsive breath he says the police were stupid. Obama's premature comments were stupid! The later "beer summit" added to the absurd positions Obama had taken.

3---   At a press conference, when asked about the justice department's dubious (perhaps stupid) gun running project to Mexican drug lords (FAST AND FURIOUS), Obama said he couldn't comment because the investigation was not complete, but he couldn't resist the premature comment that his attorney general would never have approved the program. And yet, Slippery Eric Holder actually had! Once again, the Obama approach of READY---FIRE---AIM.

4---   Obama and his Attorney General Holder suddenly, impulsively declare that Khalid Sheik Muhammad (KSM), 9/11 mastermind and other 9/11 Islamist killers, will be tried in Manhattan and Obama says, not to worry, they will eventually be executed anyway. The Obama comments could be used by any smart lawyer to declare a mistrial because of tainted jury pools. Obama taught law?

5---   Obama and his team try to down-play Dr. Hassan's Islamist terror jihad murders at Fort Hood, Texas and the Christmas Day underwear bomber's terror attempt as isolated events for local law enforcement to handle. Later, the truth emerges. Obama consistently refused to condemn Islamo-fascist murderers or use the descriptive term

Radical Muslim Terrorists. This declaration would have helped truly moderate Muslims stand firm against perversions of Islam! Dr. Hassan is a Muslim fanatic terrorist!

6--- Obama sets a deadline for Iran to stop its nuclear terror machine, but long after Obama's weak threats and pseudo deadlines, Iran proceeds with nukes and missiles at the same time as insulting our president.

7--- Young people are shot to death on the streets of Tehran protesting the evil Iranian mullahs yet Obama barely criticizes the brutal regime out of some vague hope for negotiations with the religious dictators in Iran.

8--- Syria and Iran provide missiles to Hamas and Hezbollah and Obama says nothing except to snub and criticize Israel! Obama bows to Iran and verbally insults and attacks Israel and George Bush.

9--- With illegal aliens and drugs pouring across our border with Mexico and the Democrats having ignored former President George W Bush's sound guest worker ideas years ago, now impulsive Obama ignorantly puts down Arizona's desperate effort to do what Obama won't, i.e. send troops to PROTECT OUR BORDER. Obama's homeland security secretary, Janet Napolitano and his incompetent Attorney General Holder have not even read the Arizona law they are fiercely criticizing! Unbelievable! Does Holder need remedial reading tutoring? Obama's Under Secretary of State Michael Posner makes stammering apologies to Chinese officials about Arizona's law! Janet Napolitano, our Homeland Security Czar, hadn't even read the bill either.

10--- In wake of the Gulf oil spill disaster, Obama blames Bush oil policies, BP, and off-shore drilling that he recently advocated! And all this before the situation is fully investigated by his own commission. He tries to prematurely ban all off-shore drilling which would cause thousands of lost jobs! After two judges reversed his ill-advised order, Obama stubbornly persists in his destructive behavior toward our US oil industry.

11--- Attorney General Eric Holder accuses Americans of being cowards about *our racism*. Holder is the indecisive one! He, in cowardly fashion, dropped the charges against two black panthers who intimidated voters and poll watchers with clubs in Philadelphia. One of these same men spewed hate speech on a Philadelphia street and advocated the killing of white people and their babies! This clearly coincided with the Association of Community Organizations for Reform Now (ACORN)'s illegal registering of thousands of voters to help Obama get elected. Obama and Holder have been silent about this black-power hate speech by the new Black Panthers. Racism accusations should go both ways.

12--- In reference to the proposed building of a Muslim Mosque near the new World Trade Center, Obama lectured us via teleprompter that Muslims have religious freedom in America and can build a mosque and 'cultural' center wherever they please if within the law. Then after an outcry by Americans who are finally paying attention to the placement of this Mosque, Obama dances with words about Wisdom----which he still has not gained himself! READY---FIRE---AIM again.

13--- Obama has said nothing about the threat and danger of the Mexican Drug Lords who kill, terrorize and behead Mexican authorities. Obama has also said nothing about Americans murdered by illegal aliens or drug smugglers. He sent a tiny group of US clerical and technical soldiers to the border but has not visited the border himself. His sycophants like Napolitano say the border is safer than ever.

14--- Obama has said nothing about Illinois and New York's refusal to make sure US soldiers' votes are effectively received from overseas.

15--- Obama has said almost nothing about N. Korea's aggression or the tepid Chinese response. If N. Korea attacks S. Korea again will he dither once more before acting? Obama acted as if it was either total nuclear war or doing nothing. He never considered any middle ground solutions.

16--- Obama claims to be a Christian. Why has he not spoken out about the horrendous persecution and assassinations of Christians in Iraqi churches, Cairo churches, Nigerian churches and communities? The agnostic and atheistic ranks of the mainstream media have not even chided Obama over his silence about the persecution of Christians in Muslim countries. Is it because Obama bows and scrapes to Muslims? Even those "Moderate Muslims" are either too cowardly to speak out about their murdering brothers and sisters or are vicariously glad to see Americans hurt or killed. Are we losing our RELIGIOUS WAR against radical Muslims because our own leader won't even defend fellow Christians?

17--- Obama's Appointed Head of the Joint Chiefs of our Military (General Martin Dempsey) foolishly chides Israel about planning an attack on Iran's nuclear sites. Leon Panetta, a longtime Democratic operative, uses paradoxical intention on Israel and America by foolishly, publicly implying that Israel is going to launch an attack soon on Iran. These public posturings aid and embolden Iran's aggression and further weaken our bond with Israel which paradoxically causes Arabs and Persians to further lose respect for American strength.

18--- Obama and his generals in Afghanistan foolishly apologize repeatedly for an honest, innocent mistake of burning some Muslim books! Yet some Korans had messages to Taliban insurgents from military prisoners written in them. This is contrary to Sharia Law which advises that such effaced Korans be burned. When bloody riots against American and NATO troops and assassinations of US advisors occur, our short-sighted president launches another of his apology tours. On the surface this is intended to be taking the noble high ground. However, it dilutes logic and the truth and really plays into the hands of corrupt fundamentalist Taliban propaganda. Taliban and Al Qaeda agents have long been trying to destroy NATO efforts to train Afghan police and military.

OBAMA'S CHARISMATIC HOLD OVER AMERICANS

Thoughts by Peter Olsson

I wonder where the beginnings of America's search for, and acceptance of, a new Messianic-like leader originated. I believe I can trace the quest to the painful assassinations of the Kennedy brothers, John and Robert, and Dr. Martin Luther King Jr. These were furthered by the pain of the Vietnam War and Watergate. Those losses for America were never fully grieved and mourned and allowed focus on an escalating disillusionment in older, White father-figure.

Now, along comes a charismatic, charming, smiling, speechifying mulatto man who has a vague, poorly vetted and poorly documented past, childhood and political record. Like Franz the gardener in Jersey Kosinski's novel *Being There*, Obama can be anything an adoring young or older person can make of him in their imaginings. He clearly is a devoted father, husband, Black, White, both or neither. He does pick a white older man for VP who plays a buffoon to BHO's alleged brilliance so says Obama's adoring consigliere, Valery Jarret. Such a man and his minions charisma does make.

Further to the above, I have observed that Obama gives ambiguous speeches to our country. For example, he began one speech with bromides about maintaining order but he implied falsely that America is inflicted with racist distortions of the criminal justice system. That assertion is overly exaggerated in 2014.

Obama listed issues that hamper young black Americans with an emphasis on poverty,

unemployment and underlining the 'defective' criminal justice system that he and his AG have directed over the last six years! Obama narcissistically cited his efforts in the Illinois Senate to employ videotapes of juvenile offenders being processed by the courts implying, as Bill Ayers did in his book, that teens were unjustly handled by the courts in Chicago. Ayers and Obama both NEVER MENTION THE KEY FACTOR namely that young black Americans never or rarely experience the influence, or mentoring presence of their fathers!

I predict that until Obama fully confronts his own absent father and those of young black Americans, we will not see resolution of BLACK RAGE and OBAMA'S

RAGE at America and in America.

Letter from Olsson to Messner

Larry

Since the early 1990s Al Qaeda, the Muslim brotherhood of Egypt (Zawahiri

et.al.) and the early forms of ISIS, now ISIL, grew as Lebanon, Jordon, Israel and even Cyprus have been added as countries to be dominated by WORLD WIDE Muslim ISLAMO-FACISM. On pp51-53 of my 2007 book THE CULT OF OSAMA, I cite sources documenting my summary of Al Qaeda Inc's 30 year plan to dominate the world under a Caliphate and Sharia law. Osama, Turabi, Zawahiri, et. al. met openly. Zawahiri toured the USA to talk about these plans at US mosques. As far as I can tell, Worldwide Muslim Islamo-fascism is right on schedule. The Saudi's condemn it but secretly fund ISIS.

Yesterday, a defensive defense Secretary Ash Carter talked barely coherently about what a new and terrifying danger ISIS was: well organized politically, well- funded, and having an effective army. He said we need to be planning carefully to contain them. Eric Holder and his golf-playing boss wanted to track down the beheading ISIS soldier and bring him to justice in a US court!

As Charles Krauthammer says, "That is like FDR sending out US Marshals to arrest the pilots of the planes that bombed Pearl Harbor." Hagel said we have never seen the likes of ISIS brutality. When he was serving in Nam did he not see what the Viet Cong did? The Japanese or Hitler's goons? The Khmer Rouge in Cambodia and their "Killing Fields"? I hope Hegel, Holder and Obama watched the beheading tape, but I suspect they did not.

The following letter was sent to President Obama in response to this situation by Dr. Olsson.

Mr. Obama ---we are at war with a vicious enemy who claim their God Allah is with them and you attempt to shame them by your speechifying! You say that History will not allow their success-

--But, like Hitler, Mussolini and Togo---someone had to stand up to them to help History's decision!

Dr. Peter A. Olsson

Larry's Response to Pete's Email

You could not be more correct regarding both Obama's and Holder's response to the build-up of Islamic terrorist organizations. Dithering by Obama shows a genuine lack of leadership. He simply does not understand the ramifications of the growing strength and dangerousness of ISIS. He chooses to use the term ISIL as he thinks the term includes a much larger area than just Iraq and Syria, which ISIS implies. By saying ISIL, he is recognizing the Islamic terrorists design to create a caliphate from Egypt to Iran which, incidentally, does not include Israel.

I think Obama has a genuine dislike, and even, possibly, hatred of Israel and certainly Netanyahu. I do not know what is in Obama's mind or heart, but his actions make me think he is very anti-Semitic and, possibly, based on his upbringing, even a closet Muslim and not just a Muslim lover. Regardless, he is dissing our most coveted ally in the Middle East and its only true Democracy. Obama plays a dangerous game at both Israel's and our expense.

Larry

Further thoughts by Olsson.

I agree with Obama that the defeat of Muslim Islamofascism will take a coalition but like Eisenhower and Churchill and FDR, it takes strong decisive leadership with all options on the table. **It should start with a declaration of war against ISIS by congress.**

At least Martin Dempsey the head of the joint chiefs observed that Muslim Islamo-fascism, as I prefer to call it, is in Indonesia, Yemen, Somalia and Nigeria, in the Boko Haram form, not to mention the breeding grounds in Libya and other areas of North Africa. They are definitely not a JayVee Team as Obama called them.

To use a golf analogy, Obama is driving the ball out of bounds and has a string of double bogies lined up. He keeps saying that Iraq must organize politically and militarily to defeat ISIS. Perhaps in some parts of Iraq but the Iraqi military alone can't do it for US as the danger from ISIS goes way beyond Iraq and Syria. It even means securing our border completely and knowing who is in our country. It means a "Who flies, and no fly" lists as well as passport/visa vigilance. Mr. Obama, it also means inviting our allies to meet and make war plans and quit saying, "no boots on the ground" and "No mission-creep" when everyone in the world knows

we are more than on a limited humanitarian mission. And please, don't tell the enemy when we are leaving!

Olsson's Letter to President Obama

Mr. Obama

Americans are not war weary and war wary when the mission is clear, and the leadership and policy, decision-making is clear and strong. Only 2-3% of American's are in the military who as you are quick to say---serve US well. The rest of us who pay our taxes rather see a secure border, no illegal immigration, and a clear WAR strategy to destroy ISIL---than to give free stuff, unemployment money, and food stamps to those who don't really need it.

Peter Olsson

Email from Pete to Larry

I have spent a lot of time thinking about the process of POLITICAL **LYING**. I don't know much about politicians in general, but a friend helped me to understand our Liar-in-chief. My friend points out that Obama was raised in Muslim culture and likely is familiar with Islam's acceptance of lying to achieve a righteous (?) end that serves Allah.

The Muslim term my friend describes is called "Tagiyya" (Saying something that isn't true) and/or "Kitman" (lying by omission) as a means of lying to infidels without fear of committing sin.

With Obama I think this domain reigns in many of his pronouncements ncluding his refusal to give info about his own educational financing and college grades, and, I think, even his saying that he is a Christian for mainly political purposes. His "Kitman" arena is all over his inactions in not protecting Christians and his military decision-making.

PO

These thoughts lead further into a discussion of Leadership and Trust by Larry Messner as noted below.

TRUST, LEADERSHIP and BARACK OBAMA

By Larry Messner

I have been a leader in practice since 1970, and have been reading about it, researching it and teaching it since 1977. The more I learn and read the more I see a total lack of effective leadership traits in Obama. And the first missing trait is trust. Trust is the single most important value in any relationship in order for that relationship to work properly and effectively. Once trust is broken it is almost impossible to get it back. This is true of both personal and professional relationships.

But what, exactly, does "trust" mean. It is comprised of many components, some of which I would like to elucidate here. In one explanation, trust consists of five components.

The first is **integrity**. According to Stephen Covey, American author, educator and businessman, "Integrity is conforming reality to our words – in other words, keeping promises and fulfilling expectations."

https://www.azquotes.com/quote/588123?ref=integrity

How does Obama match up with this definition? Does he always do what he says he is going to do? Does his behavior match his words? The most obvious, and recent, example is this. "If you like your healthcare plan, you'll be able to keep your healthcare plan. Period!" This was followed up with the rollout of the plan and as of today, over five million people have had their plans cancelled with an estimated 50-100 million more being threatened to have their plans cancelled next year. Did Obama know this? He says he did not.

The second component is **Responsibility**. "Hubert Selby, Jr, American writer, says in one of his best known novels, "Requiem for a Dream", "Eventually we all have to accept full and total responsibility for our actions, everything we have done, and have not done."

https://www.goodreads.com/quotes/tag/responsibility

Without going into complete detail, I think we all know how Obama blamed everyone else (Bush mostly) in his early years for Obama's failure to improve the economy. Then there is Fast and Furious, Benghazi (a video tape), the IRS and NSA (I didn't know about any of this) and, of course, Obamacare. At a meeting yesterday at the White House, apparently Obama is now going to blame the insurance companies for cancelling the millions of policies even though the insurance companies were simply following the Obamacare law. And Obama is further trying to deceive and hide as he no longer wants to call it Obamacare. More failure to take responsibility.

The third component of trust is **Understanding**.

"Any fool can know. The point is to understand." is a quote attributed to Albert Einstein. https://www.goodreads.com/quotes/tag/understanding

Does anyone truly think Obama understands how Americans feel about his Obamacare? How about Obama's understanding of Joe the Plumber and his concerns? Or how about how belittling Obama was towards Senator John McCain at their meeting soon after Obama took office? Does he ever show understanding, or does he, rather, show contempt for anyone who disagrees with him? I suggest the latter.

A fourth component of trust is **Security**.

"We welcome change and openness; for we believe that freedom and security go together, that the advance of human liberty can only strengthen the cause of world peace" This quote comes from another former President, Ronald Reagan, who said it in the "Quest for Peace, the Cause of Freedom"

https://www.goodreads.com/quotes/tag/security?page=2

Does anyone feel safe and secure with Obama as President? Do you think Netanyahu feels secure? Has Obama developed a sense of security with anyone in the Middle East? Did Ambassador Stephens and the three former seals feel secure in their final moments in Benghazi? Do you think our border guards/agents on our southern border feel secure? Do our troops in Afghanistan feel secure with Obama's rules of engagement which require them to be receiving fire from an enemy before they can shoot to defend themselves?

A final component of trust is **Time**.

"Trust has to be earned, and should come only after the passage of time." This quote comes from the champion tennis player, Arthur Ashe.

http://www.quoteambition.com/best-trust-quotes-trust-issues/"

Well, it has been almost six years of Obama's, so called, leadership. In those six years has he developed trust from you? Is he deserving of your trust? Has he lived up to even one of the above components, let alone all of them, to earn your trust?

Let me close my essay here with some quotes about trust.

Trust is "the key way to avoid being viewed with suspicion; as such, trust reflects the essence of ethics and integrity." Stephen M. R. Covey, 2008.

"Leadership is built on trust; extraordinary leadership is built on extraordinary trust; extraordinary trust is built on a leader's adherence to shared tenets of personal morality." Theodore Roosevelt

"Nearly all men can stand adversity, but if you want to test a man's character, give him power"

— Abraham Lincoln

"I am different from [George] Washington; I have a higher, grander standard of principle. Washington could not lie. I can lie, but I won't."

— Mark Twain

So, I close with the sad realization that Obama, unlike Mark Twain, or these other great leaders, has chosen to fail to develop trust through his own deliberate actions.

Larry Messner

Pete's Response to Larry's Short Discussion

Thank you, Larry, for a clear, cogent and prescient assessment of Obama and leadership.

Pete

Barack Obama's Charm and Charisma;A Psychoanalyst's View

Peter A. Olsson MD

The young confident president trots to the lectern.

His chin juts skyward as the teleprompter begins.

A charming glowing grin is his wordless preamble.

His relaxed empathy defines pure political power.

The baritone voice seeks to claim America's heartbeat.

A studied intonation resembles Martin, Billy and John.

Economic nobility is offered to scared collective souls.

The crowd's eyes aglow with adoration…mesmerized.

American sheep have found their charismatic shepherd.

THE WONDER AND MAGIC CHARM OF WORDS*

Psychoanalysts view speech acquisition as a decisive step in the foundation of the executive domain of the human mind. In this sense a child's earliest speech is a magic charm. It is directed toward forcing the external world and fate to do those things that have been conjured up in words. The child's words will continue to be important later, even when the early omnipotent magic is gradually tempered by reality. It is a serious question as to whether Obama has had such a reality check yet. Below is a telling quote from Obama.

*"I spent the last two years of high school in a daze, locking away the questions that life seemed insistent on imposing. I kept playing basketball, attended classes sparingly, drank beer heavily, and tried drugs enthusiastically. I discovered that it didn't make any difference if you smoked reefer in the white class mates sparkling new van, or in the dorm room with some brother you'd met down at the gym, or on the beach with a couple of Hawaiian kids who had dropped out of school and now spent most of their time looking for an excuse to brawl."

That's from Obama's book "Dreams from My Father" describing **HIS** high school and college days.

The Developmental Roots of Charm/Charisma

Charm may have as its earliest origin in the smile response that occurs normally at three or four months of human development. A wonderful charming smile helps caretakers to bond in delight with the infant. Some infants more than others, have the gift of more glowing smiles. In the Darwinian sense, the smile reduces any potential propensity to destroy or harm the innocent infant by a stranger. Barack Obama's smile says volumes before he ever says a word. Obama's boyish charm has helped him survive a difficult childhood. It also helped create and sustain his dazzlingly rapid ascendance to political power.

Even as a chubby toddler Barack Obama possessed a winning smile and early gift with and command of words. His white grandmother who Obama calls Tut (pronounced toot), though not without reasons, that young Barack was a genius...especially with words.

David Maraniss, in his book about Obama, describes Barack's comment as the English class of Ms. Czurles-Nelson at Punahou School discussed **what people fear the most.**

Obama said, that words are to be feared, whether used personally or internationally can be destructive weapons.

As I observe Obama's verbal skills in action, it is impressive how he entwines graceful movements, a winsome smile, and a smooth charm that accompanies his powerful wielding of words. His verbal-based charisma is significantly connected to the timing of his rising and falling baritone intonations. These seem studied and resemble other influential speakers like Bill Clinton, Martin Luther King, John Kennedy, Billy Graham, et. al.

Barack Obama Jr. however, seems spellbound by the omnipotent fantasy of the imagined pure power of his words. As if the programs he would establish, and their successful results were already on record. How could anyone disagree with the smooth magic of his words? What could account for such sincere and benevolent conviction about the omnipotence of Obama's use of words?

Barack Obama, like all of us, has a personality structure formed over many years. How can Barack Obama's Personality be described? How do his charm and charisma interfuse with his personality and self- development?

I believe Obama's unique disorder of the self is best described as an 'AS IF" Personality, a variant of what has recently been called Narcissistic Personality Disorder.

BACKGROUND: PSYCHOANALYTIC THEORY APPLIED TO OBAMA

In 1934, and again in 1942, Helene Deutsch described what she called the "As If" personality type. She was referring to individuals who leave other people with an impression of inauthenticity, even though they seem to enjoy "normal" relations with those around them and even though they complain of no disorder. They appear perfectly well adjusted and are even capable of a certain warmth, but in several circumstances they betray a lack of emotional depth.

The apparently normal relationship to the world corresponds to a child's imitativeness and is the expression of identification with the environment, a mimicry which results in an ostensibly good adaptation to the world of reality but on the surface. Their creations are, on observation, rehearsed for effect. Another characteristic of the 'as if' personality is that aggressive tendencies are almost completely covered by passivity Obama's verbal aggression leads to an air of negative goodness on the surface. Obama can quietly be ruthless in gaining political ascendancy. That is of course how he seems to govern, for what he thinks is the peoples' own good. And HIS ends seems to justify the means.

Obama's perpetual search for his father-himself is a constant self-creation resulting in his endless perception of himself as a self-appointed omnipotent father-parent-illusionary transformative messiah.

Barack Obama's "AS-IF" ness of personality leads to a chameleon-like quality that allows him at a surface level to swiftly relate to many people in an amiable, apparently empathic, manner. This attribute is helpful at campaign events but in the on-going relationships with hard-nosed Republicans and bureaucrats, Obama seems to quickly grow bored, haughty or insulting. He talks about bipartisan collaboration but has little patience for those who differ from his views. Obama like most fragile Narcissists are trapped in the confines of their own wonderfulness. They play well only with others who adore them and agree with them.

Some Psychodynamic Speculations about Obama's Development of Self:

During his childhood years Obama experienced repeated painful separations, abandonments, disappointments and geographic relocations. Obama summoned up valiant efforts to defend himself against these traumas and he adapted remarkably well to changes of parental figures and social-cultural circumstances. In his memoir *Dreams From My Father*, Obama conveys with poignant literary skill a genuine search for his father-himself. His political career seems to have been a continuation of his personal heroic identity myth. He lived this out with the clients he served as a community organizer and Illinois senator. His ultimate focus remains on his grandiose self-discovery and a fusion of this with his utopian Robin Hood-like policies and promises.

Part of Obama's identity discovery process was his unique ability to empathize with people of different cultures and points of view. This helped him build significant friendships in high school and college. Like his mother, his inner anthropologist always seemed to allow an emotional distance, objectivity and detachment.

Some friends who grew very close to Obama experienced this as a "coldness".

Genevieve Cook lived with Obama for a year when he studied at Columbia University in 1984. She clearly loved Barack Obama but noticed a distance and coldness about him. Genevieve in her diary says,

> "I am feeling anger at him for some reason, multi-stranded reasons. His warmth can be deceptive. Though he speaks sweet words and can be open and trusting, there is also that – coolness—and I begin to have an inkling of some things about him that could get to me"

She pictures Obama acting out a superhero legend, in a way Hemingway could describe. (Maraniss, D. (2012) Barack Obama: The Story).

Just as his father Barack Obama Sr. sought to rescue and obtain economic salvation for his native Kenya, Barack Obama Jr. seems to search for the same for America. Father and son both glory in the magic power of their words. They both possessed/possess various forms of charm and charisma. They both seem destined however, to discover the limitations of any one person's words, charm, or charisma. Therein lies Obama's tragic flaw.

Larry, I have some further detailed background thoughts on Obama and his narcissism.

In 1971 (Over 40 years ago now!) Heinz Kohut in his writings, *The Analysis of the Self* (1971) and his essay (1978) *Creativeness, Charisma, Group Psychology*, published in *The Search For the Self*, developed the concept he called Self-Psychology". Self-Psychology is an extension of classic psychoanalysis. The majority of Kohut's patients were psychiatrists, psychologists and psychoanalysts whose first or prior analyses or therapies had been unsuccessful. His customers were all highly successful people but suffered from a subtle inner emptiness, coolness and detachment. Their friends, colleagues and spouses became aware slowly over time of their narcissistic cocoon. As expected, their relationships were unhappy and strangely shallow, detached and they were experienced by others as distant and easily bored.

Kohut is difficult to read because of his long Germanic complex sentences, but, his work has been extremely valuable. Particularly, I think for an understanding of Barack Obama, his "As If" variety of Narcissistic Personality has taken keen observers many years to detect. Some of the public has just begun to register the implications of Obama's personality for American domestic and foreign policy.

I believe the Obamacare debacle has been the psychological straw that has broken the back of Obama's psychological camel. There have been many other scandals, failures of Obama policy, and leadership. Some are glaring, and his dithering, procrastinatory decision – making fiascos have led to narcissistic injuries for Obama. Additionally, the health care debacle and sad child immigrants on our southern border hit home deeply into Obama's narcissistic core.

When a narcissistic personality begins to decompensate they do not go psychotic like a paranoid or borderline personality disorder. Rather, the narcissist begins to show what Kohut called subtle fragmentations of the self. Like Obama they grow rigid, aloof, arrogant, haughty and irritable, sometimes grandiose.

In Obama's case I would predict that his speeches and interviews become more and more self-absorbed and grandiose. But, the form his speeches will take is more of a rescue for poor down-trodden Americans that his policies have actually made worse. Obama will talk more and more about income redistribution, anti- white racism and economic unfairness in American capitalism just as his father attacked Kenyan capitalism many years ago. He will emphasize intense scapegoating of conservative Republican demons and those in the Supreme Court who disagree with the emperor.

The biggest danger I think, is Obama's wishful bonding efforts with Putin and Iran when they betray his peace efforts. It is even possible that more of our embassies and even our homeland could be subject to real and cyber-attacks. Further, deeper narcissistic levels of rage will be seen in Obama. Unlike Bush 41 and Bush 43, Obama has no support group around him except sycophants.

More later---Pete Olsson

Some Thoughts in an Email from Pete to Larry

OBAMAS' CONTEMPT and, CONTEMPT for OBAMA

In our opinion, CONTEMPT seems to be the crucial underlying theme of Barack Obama and Eric Holder. Contempt for the constitution, contempt for the congress, contempt for our military and ultimately, contempt for America. Holder was actually found in contempt! Obamaism is a clever interweaving of Saul Alinsky's "Rules for Radicals" and Obama's Neo Marxist theology of utopian global "social justice"; as defined by Obama the Pied Piper and philosopher King of "Hope and Change.

A vivid example of Obama's contempt for America was his swap of the five Islamist mastermind monsters for traitor Bergdahl. This ill-conceived trade was the height of foolishness and possibly stems from his stubborn and misguided efforts to close GITMO before he leaves office. It also deflects from the medical disasters at the Veterans' Administration, Benghazi blood-gate, IRS scandal, Fast and Furious, and other scandals. Not to mention the increased danger of kidnapping of Americans all over the world.

At an unconscious level the Obamas have always intended to bring America down a peg or two, especially our economy. For the good of HIS America, he seeks to destroy, or at least greatly diminish, the Republican party and free market capitalism.

Now, America's Contempt for Obama will proceed.

Peter Olsson

Larry's Response to Pete

Pete, you are totally correct. Let's look at how Obama differs in his handling of a U.S. Serviceman in captivity. On the one hand, he is willing to trade five of the worst terrorist leaders to get back one deserter. By the way I used to run the AWOL/Deserter Program for the U.S. Air Force at Westover AFB. After being gone, with no rationale, for 24 hours you are declared AWOL. If you stay gone for 30 days, you are converted to deserter status. Bergdahl is a deserter, Period.

Comparatively the Marine, Tahmooressi, a valid hero as defined by his comrades in arms, is held captive for absolutely no reason by our "friends" the Mexican government for over two months and Obama can't even find the time to call the Mexican President and tell him, as I would have, that he has 24 hours to return the Marine or Mexico will be put off limits to all Americans and all trade will stop and all foreign trade and aid will end. I would also sail a U.S. Naval Carrier task force up to the Mexican coast and do a few low-level flyovers of the Mexican President's home and office. Maybe at supersonic speed so the sonic boom will get his attention.

This is truly an interesting juxtaposition. On the one hand, the prisoner swap damages all Americans for years to come. Even Obama says that "absolutely" these freed terrorists may come back to harm us. Like he cares? No, he clearly has no regard for the safety of our country and our fellow Americans. He should be impeached. Both Nixon and Clinton did little in comparison. One was shamed out of office and the other, who has no shame, was impeached. But this president is guilty of what Article II, Section 4 of the Constitution says about reasons for impeachment, namely "...other high Crimes and Misdemeanors".

To further explain, there have been many impeachments of federal officers (president, cabinet officer, senator and judges) since 1787. Each of the impeachments involved charges of misconduct incompatible with the official position of the officeholder. This conduct falls into three broad categories: (1) exceeding the constitutional bounds of the powers of the office in derogation of the powers of another branch of government; (2) behaving in a manner grossly incompatible with the proper function and purpose of the office; and (3) employing the power of the office for an improper purpose or gain.

I believe you can make a case against Obama for each of these three reasons. 1. He is usurping the powers of congress by his edicts, most recently the trade of the terrorists. 2. He daily behaves in a manner that violates the function and purpose of his office, both by action and inaction and 3. He employs his office for gaining power as a dictator.

I would impeach him today. Period!

Larry Messner

Further to the Above Email by Larry

The reason Bergdahl got promoted in absentia is because the Pentagon designated him as a POW, which he wasn't. He was a hostage of the Haqanni group and therefore not entitled to promotions. A Pentagon spokesperson said that, although they "suspected" he deserted, they had no proof! Their first clue should have been that when he left the base, he did so while leaving behind his rifle, night vision goggles and his bulletproof vest. They also had his platoon members telling them that he deserted but they ignored them. Shameful.

Additionally, someone said on TV yesterday that once a new rank is given, it can't be revoked! My Lord they think we're stupid. Military personnel are "busted back" every day....and that needs to happen here.

Larry

"NEW" OBAMA CHARACTERISTICS---STUBBORN DEFIANCE AND ARROGANCE

Recently at his state of the union speech Obama showed increasing denial about the recent election and its implications. He proceeded with his same secular progressive speech and seemed to find pleasure in defying Republicans at every turn. His denial of the reality of our national debt is impressive. His dressing-down of the SCOTUS at the state of the union speech was revolting and arrogant. Clearly, those Americans who don't have to assume the burden of the debt and will benefit from its largesse worship Obama as their Robin Hood hero.

Peter Olsson

Further Email from Peter to Larry

Obama's Saul Alinsky-worshipping when combined with Black Liberation theology (A la Rev. Jeremiah Wright Jr.), represents the final emergence of Obama's expression of his true self. Our anger at Obama is, I think, a normal reaction to his own angry defiance. Obama never expressed his true feelings until after he got re-elected. Most all of us had such fond hopes when Obama gave his eloquent speech at the Democrat convention before his first campaign and his first inaugural speech. But what has gradually emerged has been a progression from underlying CONTEMPT for America, our founding fathers, and his version of the Constitution. But he wasn't alone in his contempt for America as both his wife, Michelle, and the Rev Wright, his pastor of over 20 years, have also expressed their contempt. Michelle was only first proud of America once her husband had been elected President and Rev Wright thought God should damn America and even said it was in the Bible.

Then since his re-election, stubborn defiance and further contempt have been embodied by Eric Holder's divisive race-baiting.

A final observation concerns Obama's adolescent rebellion against even normal, helpful religious, political and law enforcement authority. He, like millions of Americans, mistakenly confuse sick fundamentalist religious mentality and authority with the joy, tranquility and beauty of God's grace as expressed in Jesus's love.

Pete

Larry's Response to Pete

Excellent points all, Pete. I have felt Obama's contempt and disdain for America ever since he said on Oct 30, 2008, just before the election, that "We are five days away from fundamentally transforming the United States of America". That immediately raised a lot of questions for me. Like, what needs fundamentally transforming about our beloved country? Sure there are issues to be dealt with but when you say fundamentally, you are saying down to the core. Was he saying we need to shred our Constitution and Declaration of Independence and start all over?

And I don't think it was an accident that his wife, Michelle, said, as reported in a Newsweek article on Mar 12, 2018 by Evan Thomas, that ""For the first time in my adult life, I am really proud of my country because it feels like hope is finally making a comeback." It has been my experience that married couples normally reflect each other's opinions which is one reason they remain married. So, I don't find it unusual that President Obama may feel similarly as his wife, Michelle, with regards to America.

And what was he thinking he wanted to fundamentally transform our country in to? A Socialist-Progressive-Marxist regime? As time is showing, I believe that is exactly what he wants to do.

Larry

And Another Email from Pete to Larry

Larry

In recent times Obama's speeches and appearances have clearly involved his intense, even desperate efforts to deflect from the unresolved scandals of his incompetent administration, and his incompetent handling of foreign affairs. Obama's non- war or tepid war on Violent Global Muslim Islamist Fascism and its attack on Western Judeo-Christian culture and our citizens is worrisome.

ISIS's huge grabs of territory and the religious devotion and dedication of ISIS, Al Qaeda, Taliban, Hamas, and Hezbollah followers is best not under estimated. Obama seems to deny the exponential "Existential" **and spiritual threat** that ISIS poses to U.S. Obama's outer arrogance, "Mr. Coolness" and cockiness I think covers over his inadequate assessment of ISIS, et. Al. The more Obama faces accurate and broad-ranging flaws in his decision-making, foreign policy judgment, and disorganized administrative follow-up procedures...the more arrogant, haughty, stubborn and defiant he becomes.

PO

Larry's Letter to President Obama

Dear President Obama,

To paraphrase your wife, Michelle, for the first time in my life I am ashamed to be an American. You have diminished us in the eyes of the world through your actions regarding the threat from Islamic Radical Terrorists. While not all Muslims are terrorists, most terrorists are Muslims. Your refusal to even recognize what is happening in the world and label the terrorist properly is preventing you from creating a strategy to defeat them. You admit you have no strategy. Wake up Mr. President. Open your eyes to the barbarism being committed by these Islamic terrorists. You are so quick to condemn Christians from 1,000 years ago but can't condemn the Islamic threat today. Even the Islamic terrorists say they are having a religious war with the Christians, Jews and all those who don't accept their form of Islam.

I gave almost 24 years of my life in the U.S. Air Force defending this country and you are now "fundamentally transforming" it into a third world country. Shame on you. Grow up and become a leader who will stand up for America and all her past greatness.

Laurence F. Messner, Lt Col, USAF (Retired)

Pete's Email to Larry

As I continue to explore the Snopes subtle scandal, I wonder if Snopes, like the increasingly left-wing New York Times, will join the major networks in down-playing John Kerry's unproductive egoistic and narcissistic obsession with achieving a nuclear treaty with Iran at any price to America. I have not noted any mention of Kerry's consultations made with Condi Rice, Jim Baker, or even Colin Powell. Kerry's going it alone worries me almost as much as Obama's stubborn defiance of and obnoxiousness towards Republicans and Israel.

Susan Rice and Samantha Powers, like Obama and Kerry, worship at the altar of the fantasied power of words at speeches and their own egos. I think the insulting, unwelcoming of Netanyahu by Obama and some Democrats demonstrates how shaky and weak Obama's treaty efforts are vis a vis Iran.

And Further My Friend

And we know, Larry, how successful Kerry and Hillary before him have been with the Israeli/Palestinian conflict, the paper tiger approach to Assad, and Kerry/Obama's ineffective professorial preaching at Putin. Obama seems to be psychologically stuck and mired-down in the simplistic thought that an approach to Iran's hidden nuclear weapons factories is either bombing or weak chummy capitulation and false hopes.

Larry, as Joe Biden would say---"This Treaty with Iran is 'a big F... ing deal'"

I doubt if Snopes approves of my thoughts---smile.

If Obamaism is defeated in 2016, then the hard work would just begin, because Obama will continue his omnipotent messiah campaign as a TV celebrity cheerleading the Obamaites to further heights of left wing perdition. Obama's community organizing will be expanded into global community organizing!!

PAO

Pete's Continued Thoughts

Obamaisms of leadership

1---Preach "Transparency"---then walk secretly and deviously.

2---Walk and talk loudly and carry a little twig.

3---Act outraged and call for an investigation about a scandal--- then lament about "Old News" years later when no investigation has been concluded.

4---Hornswoggle the electorate about how good they have it...when nothing substantial has been accomplished.

5---Knock the American people off their high horses by shaming, blaming and scolding them

About the crusades hundreds of years ago---and slavery, as if the majority aren't way beyond it.

6---Lambast and insult White Honky Republicans for obstructing, and then call for their bipartisan cooperation.

7---Decry Republican investigators about "playing politics"--- then smear them politically via your media acorn-like buddies.

8---Poorly supervise and over-see massive spending---then call-out Republicans for being cold cruel tightwads.

9---Do dictatorial, unconstitutional things with your presidential order pen---then dare congress to impeach you as a distraction.

10---Praise and complement our Troops---then refuse to listen to their leaders and put them in danger by POTUS "Rules of Engagement" and military budget cutting.

I think Obama's insults, undermining, and contempt for traditional American values are so enraging of the Republican congress, that their unconscious minds are so focused on impeaching him that they feel and act consciously as if they are hamstrung on the surface. [SAUL ALINSKY DOES A JIG IN HIS GRAVE!]

Pete Olsson

Pete Emails Larry

Larry---And what is so enraging is that Obama seems to enjoy every photo-op with military heroes yet, does little to actually help the military and quietly cuts military budgets.

Pete

Larry Writes to Pete and President Obama

Not to bore you, but I sent the following two missives to Obama in the past. By now I am convinced we will be audited by the IRS and, most likely, the NSA is bugging my emails. So, it is with great pride that I give you, and them, more to read...smile. As you can see the first email was sent when I lived in Nevada.

Dear Mr. President,

I don't know what is wrong with you, but you are anything but presidential. You are in constant campaign mode and all you do is attack, belittle and humiliate everyone who disagrees with you.

You are only leader to half of America. The other half are, in your opinion, the enemy. Most recently you commented about the Republicans "Bring it on". My god almighty. Are we your enemy? Are you ours? You sure make it appear that way.

You are the most divisive president in our history and you are driving huge wedges between Americans. I urge you to stop immediately and start growing up and acting presidential.

And please, for God's sake, stop attacking our allies (UK and Israel) while pandering to our enemies (Hugo Chavez et al) and bowing to all while apologizing endlessly.

Sincerely,

Laurence F. Messner, Lt Col, USAF (Retired)

Henderson, NV

And Another Letter to President Obama from Larry

Dear President Obama,

As a retired U.S. Air Force Lieutenant Colonel and teacher of leadership, I am abhorred and outraged by your inability to make the proper decision.

On the news last night, I saw an authorized protest taking place on the Washington, DC Mall for immigration reform. Let's understand this. While our veterans are being denied access to their own memorials on the Mall, a protest, largely for the benefit of granting illegal immigrants the right to vote and become American citizens, is being authorized and paid for by your administration. Is it because you honor law breaking illegal aliens more than your own veterans and citizens? It sure looks that way.

If there is no money to keep the veteran memorials open, (and the irony is that doing nothing would have cost nothing) where did the money come from to put up barriers and have Park Police patrol the memorials to keep veterans out? And who paid for the platform, banners, microphones and people to put up all these items?

So, the very people, our veterans, who fought for the right for free speech which this protest is using to make their protest heard, are being denied their rights.

Further, your administration has now denied benefits to the families of our fallen heroes upon the return of their remains to America. How dare you!

What is wrong with your administration? Where are your priorities? Why are you so disrespectful of veterans and our military? I put the entire blame on you. You may or may not have ordered the closing of the veteran memorials, but you certainly can open them with the stroke of a pen.

Why won't you do the right thing?

Sincerely,

Laurence F. Messner, Lt Col, USAF (Retired)

Email from Pete to Larry

Larry

I listened and looked at the Friedman interview of Obama and I found it very worshipful of Obama. The few tough follow-up questions still allowed Obama to filibuster-on in his charismatic seductive style. If a listener quickly grants Obama his questionable prophetic assumptions, historical pontifications and high-stakes then he, like Friedman, can find his arguments compelling. I don't find them compelling at all.

Obama as usual is a clever specifier and charming salesman about his "Music Man" ideas for USA and the world. He minimizes both long and short term problems with "His team's" approach. Deep-down, I think Obama wants to punt the ball till he leaves the presidency and is trying to render America a has- been power like France and England.

Further Discussions by Pete

My observations and questions are:

1---I fundamentally doubt Obama's trustworthiness, truthfulness, and leadership capacity to implement 'the deal'. Obama worships the fantasy of the power of his own words. Remember his tepid comments and inaction when freedom - seekers in Tehran were being slaughtered in the streets. He in his usual fashion made some foolish moral equivalency between the freedom fighters and the cruel theocrats.

2---I completely doubt Obama's empty reassurances about his support of Israel and his alleged and faint praise of Netanyahu. His feeling of Israel's pain comments and bogus comments about Israel's defense of itself when Gaza was raining rockets on Israel doesn't fit with his ACTIONS and inactions at the time. When Iran attacks Israel will Obama join in a counter attack or will he just give more money for their "Iron Dome"?

3---Does Obama really believe in the effectiveness and thoroughness of the inspections to verify Iran's compliance? I doubt it! Friedman barely questioned Obama via any tough follow-up questions or references to Iran's KNOWN FAILURE TO COMPLY WITH IEAE INSPECTORS. Obama slithered by that issue completely.

4---What would Obama's "Team" and our "Allies" do when Iran fudges and violates an agreement? The cows will already be out of the barn. Russia will be trading with Iran, Germany, China and Europe will be busy trading with Iran as the sanctions are phased out. US businesses will be eager to join the economic action. Or if congress increases sanctions the world will laugh at our isolationism. Obama as usual will blame Bush's legacy and Republicans.

5---What will Obama do when the sanction-free Iran has more money to sponsor its aggression and sponsoring of terror?

6---Obama keeps saying in simplistic fashion that it is either his bogus gamble on an agreement versus all-out war. I could envision many other options---SUCH AS:

a. Insist that Iran recognize Israel and agree to refrain from terror sponsorship---If they won't as a first step then increase sanctions much further and ask the UN for resolutions against Iran

b. If Iran persists---threaten focused heavy bunker-busting bombing after a deadline (Not an Obama "Red Line"!")

c. Repeat #b every six weeks until Iran complies.

d. If Iran attacks US or Israel---use a tactical nuclear bomb to emphasize our will. (Hiroshima but on the Iran Nuke facility not a city.)

Pete Olsson

Larry's Response to Pete's Further Discussions

1. Completely agree Pete. Obama prefers talk to action. At some point action will be needed as this is truly a bogus deal designed to appear to be more than it is.

2. I seriously doubt that Obama has the stomach or inclination to protect Israel from any outside attack by Iran or any other Muslim country. His contempt for Netanyahu is what leads me to this conclusion.

3. Like so many inspection programs of the past, this one, too, will lead nowhere and prove to be a false security blanket designed solely to bolster Obama's self-belief that he is the great peacemaker. (Like the bogus Nobel Peace Prize he accepted soon after his inaugural for doing nothing more than being alive.)

4. You're right. I am guessing Obama will blame Bush for everything he does wrong. Shameful leadership.

5. First Obama won't recognize any Islamic Terrorism by Iran or any other Islamic threat. If he finally wakes up to reality, the blame will go elsewhere.

6. So true. When I was stationed in Europe for seven years, I came to know about America's idea to have a strong non-nuclear military so we could respond to any Russian attack without having to immediately resort to nukes, tactical or otherwise. A strong conventional military can actually prevent a nuclear exchange. Obama's belief that it is an all or nothing approach shows his simple, naïve approach for using a military option he has no experience with. He needs to read history.

Larry

Pete's Continuing Observations and Summarizing

On another issue---The Fort Hood anniversary highlights another scandalous behavior by our Speechifier-in-chief and his military advisor minions.

My opinions below:

1---In my opinion the Fort Hood Islamist attack by Hassan was **both** workplace violence for which Hasan's superiors had responsibility **and,** an enemy attack inspired by Awlaki a radical Muslim Imam! The killed and injured at Ft. Hood deserve purple hearts and full and back pay and help for their rehabilitation. (If deserter/and treason-laden Bowe Birgdahl gets back pay and continuing salary from USA and special Rose Garden treatment by poisonous POTUS and TV praise by Susan Rice (Our insecurity advisor) ... for "Serving with distinction"! ---The Ft. Hood victims each deserve all Bowe's money and many times over!)

2---Obama to this day has not called out the radical Muslim gurus who recruit pawns like Major Hassan. Obama's denial of global radical Muslim Islamo-Fascism is scary. Obama clearly exhibits the defense mechanism of

REACTION FORMATION. a psychological defense mechanism in which one form of behavior substitutes for or conceals a diametrically opposed repressed impulse to protect against it.]

I think Obama shows a passive, idealization and worshipfulness of Islam that stems from his childhood wounds in Indonesia and influences by an Islamic school and culture. His escalating out-spoken anti-Christian talk and hostility is I think related to his decayed and feelings about Rev Wright's sick version of Christianity. Obama's denial, haughty arrogance and lack of personal awareness of his psychological blind- spots is alarming and dangerous.

3---The supervisors of physician psychiatrist at Walter Reed were incompetent and kicked the troubled Hasan can down the road when he should have been administratively separated from the Army. Hasan's horrible behavior is a soul-saddening blot on my profession.

4---Related to the above issues is Obama's empty promise to fix the VA system. All that took place seems to be the magic power Obama feels about his words. He has never governed, lead, administrated or followed up with the departments whose heads he appointed! I don't think he even plays golf with them.

Peter Olsson

Larry's Answer to Pete

Pete,

I am coming to believe that Obama simply cannot or will not assign proper blame to any Islamic attack on America anywhere, and, the scary part for me, is I believe it is because he is a closet Muslim. I have absolutely no proof of this, but I watch his actions again and again and he defends Muslims regardless of their outlandish and murderous behavior.

Larry

Pete's Email on Defeating ISIS

Obama announces his bold new plan to defeat ISIS.450 advisors to train Sunni warriors in Anbar? Over the last year or two we have only effectively trained a handful of Sunnis and Obama still refuses to directly arm the Kurds in N. Iraq in deference to the Iran puppet in Baghdad. Obama and Biden tried to declare victory in Iraq and get out without **insisting on a Status of Forces Agreement (SOFA)** with Malicki. The US, Iraq and coalition was set up for defeat by Al Qaeda and ISIS.

I think Obama's pseudo-strategy against ISIS is, as usual, too little, too late and too publicized for our enemies' eyes. Clearly Obama is temporizing until he can pass the ISIS problem to the next POTUS. Obama's strategy always has been to discredit Bush and get us out of Iraq and Afghanistan **at any price**. He also rigidly seeks to close GITMO to make US look more righteous to the world community which he fancies himself the leader, rather than America. An unintended or intended consequence of Obama's utopian Strategy is to take US military power "Down a peg" like his similar attempt to redistribute our wealth and diminish our exceptional republic.

Through stupidity or intent Obama was and is short-sighted about our wars in Iraq and Afghanistan. It was not just ousting Saddam Hussein and his WMDs or blasting the Taliban and Al Qaeda in Afghanistan and Al Qaeda which we attracted to Iraq, so we could destroy them and which we did! We also, with checkered success, tried to give both countries a taste of democracy.

And finally, we wanted to keep strong military presences in both counties like we have in Japan, Germany and other world locations in case we need to protect America and our interests. With the Putin's, Iran's and ISIS's of the world who only understand power and not "utopian reset buttons", bows and handshakes, ala Obama during his world apology tour, our superpower status and strength is the only way toward peace.

Peter Olsson

Larry's Response

I agree. But I believe that defeating ISIS is going to be a very long term process. It is like smashing a ball of Mercury on a metal anvil. It shatters and pieces go everywhere. So, did we smash ISIS or spread it around?

Sometimes I think the best idea would be to declare victory and withdraw. This MidEast conflict is never ending. It has been ongoing for millennia and will likely continue long after we depart. But it is definitely better to fight it there rather than here.

Closing GITMO is sheer idiocy. The terrorists are confined and not subject to our criminal court rules. Why provide prisoners of war with legal representation? During most wars in the past, POW's have been held captive until the conflict is over. That philosophy should apply here as well.

I agree with your idea of peace through strength. When I was in the Strategic Air Command (SAC) their motto was "Peace is our Profession". At that time the Air Force understood that a strong offensive capability led to peace. Hence, our nuclear strategy of Mutual Assured Destruction (MAD). The only problem with that strategy now is that I seriously wonder if the leaders in some of the Muslim countries really fear mass destruction, although I pray they do.

Larry

Pete's Email about Obama's Ethnicity

I sometimes wonder if Obama hates the white part of himself? I had hoped that as the first mulatto president he could bring together the very white identity of his mother and the very black identity of his father in positive and liberating ways. When he lectures, shames, scolds and chastises "White America" for what he thinks is some residual racism, he seems to think or acts like he is some deity above race. As a crude analogy he seems like the guy with dog dirt on his shoe that complains that every place he goes smells and needs air purifier.

PO

Larry's Answer

Intriguing question, Pete. He is constantly referred to as America's first black president, yet that moniker was also given to former President Bill Clinton by a fawning press. But, in reality, Obama is half white. So is he black too? Well, half anyway, which, as you have rightfully pointed out, makes him our first mulatto president, not our first black president. Of course, the term mulatto is now anathema to the word police on the left.

Larry

Pete's Query to Larry on Leadership

As a teacher and student of leadership Larry, you know, and we have discussed, that in any organization the leader at the top sets the tone. When Barack Obama became the first mulatto president I had high hopes that Obama would use his white identity from his white American mother, and his black identity from his black, Kenyan foreign exchange student father, in positive ways of leadership. Unfortunately, he has used his power and position to devalue and demean the American congress (Particularly white

Republicans...leaving black conservative congresspersons unmentioned.)

Obama also devalues and demeans the Supreme Court of America's decisions, even before they publish their decision! Obama tramples on our American Constitution which he is sworn to uphold and enforce. Obama does this by presidential orders and by refusing to enforce the laws of America.

In my current opinion, Obama hates the white part of himself at an unconscious level. Obama scolds, shames and tries to guilt-provoke Americans, black and white, who disagree with him. He implies that we are racist and poorly informed. I also don't think that he really understands black Americans who use the N... word to joke with or devalue each other as much as the small number of white racist bigots in America. Obama did know a sector of black America on the Southside of Chicago for a few years when he worked as a community organizer. Not a large sample.

I believe Obama's anger at his whiteness stems from a mother who disrupted his childhood with separations, bewildering geographic moves and her unhappy relationships with men such as his erstwhile father figures. Obama barely knew his misogynistic, alcoholic and verbose, verbally aggressive and abusive black father. Barack senior so offended faculty at Harvard that he was never granted a degree.

So, Obama harbors anger about his whiteness and his blackness. Whenever he speechifies about America's progress he invariably couples it with barbs, pokes and shaming about "how much more work needs to be done "by us Americans who unconsciously contain "Micro racist aggressions" and unresolved inter-generationally transmitted racism, left over from America's past dark history of slavery.

I think it is Obama who projects his own inner racial ambivalence and unconscious conflicts onto U.S.

Peter Olsson

Larry's Response to Pete

So, I agree with you Pete. I also believe Obama is ashamed of his white half. He can't change that, so he vilifies whites to show how black he is. A terribly sad excuse for a man and leader. I pray we escape the next 17 months somewhat intact as a nation.

Larry

Pete's Email Regarding Race Relations in America

We live in Obama's, Reid's, Pelosi's and Hillary's land of "Free Dope and Spiritual

Mange". Sad, George Washington, Thomas Jefferson and many northern leaders owned slaves. Abraham Lincoln had made racist jokes early in his personal history. If Reid and Obama would read and understand history, they would come to understand the importance of the process of reconciliation which involved many decades of successful healing in our country.

Now, the liberal progressive, neo-Marxist Utopianists are going to try to rip America apart with their smug, smarmy, politically correct, ethnic and racial cleansing. I pray that people like the evil Dylann Roof, who murdered innocent church attendees in Savannah, GA while he prayed with them, will not be successful in his desire for a race war in America.

Obama, rather than promoting healing in America as the forgiving church attendees did, is both subliminally and overtly promoting a race war in America. Unlike Mandella and MLK, I believe Obama conflates his own personal racial ambivalence about his identity with our country's. Rather than leading constructively, he provokes, shames and tries to provoke white guilt and black resentment and rage. God help America.

Pete

Larry's Comeback

Oh, how sadly right you are Pete. Race relations have deteriorated badly under this non-leader's time at the helm. America had some serious problems in the past, but far too many on the left are content to focus on and emphasize our slavery past without once acknowledging that over 600,000, mostly young white men, died during the Civil War to excoriate that shameful practice. Does America get any credit for cleansing itself? Not from the left and, apparently, not from Obama.

I don't know why that is, but I suspect it is because Progressives love to wallow in white guilt instead of moving forward and contributing to the healing process. Leaders have a responsibility to lead from the front and set the tone and culture of any organization they lead. Sadly, Obama is doing exactly that, but in the wrong direction.

Larry

Pete's Beliefs on Mid East Involvement and Islamofascism

I find it helpful to review the original reasons for our US led coalition's reasons for invading Iraq:

1---The removal of Saddam Hussein who violated numerous UN resolutions and fired at our allied aircraft enforcing the no-fly zone, mass murdered of his own citizens with poisoned gas and other weapons of mass destruction and tortured his political opponents and cruelly ruled his country. French, British and US Intelligence presented strong intelligence that Saddam sought an active nuclear program. John Kerry, Hillary Clinton and other congressional leaders strongly urged and supported Bush 43 to act militarily in Iraq as well as Afghanistan where Al Qaeda originally grew strong under the Taliban's protection.

2---Establish an ally and base in the Middle East from which future 9/11 type terror events could be prevented and al Qaeda training bases could be destroyed. In fact, Abu Musab al- Zarqawi the original ISIS warrior and recruiter was killed in Iraq where he led his trainees from Afghanistan to do beheadings, bombings and assassinations in Iraq. It can be strongly argued that efforts to establish democracies in Afghanistan and Iraq had the two-pronged benefit a) Helping reduce future needs for ISIS, Al Qaeda, Muslim Brotherhood et.al. to seek to govern with sharia law and Islamofascism governments and b) Keeping Al Qaeda, ISIS and other Islamists "Busy" and on the defense OVER THERE and not attacking here or in Western Europe.

3---Secure oil in Iraq and protect western oil interests in general. We even have bought oil from Iraq and not just taken it as 'spoils ' of war.

4---In my opinion, Americans who mistakenly supported and still support Obama's foolish promotion of glib war weariness, and too quick to completely withdraw "Boots" from both Iraq and Afghanistan have unfortunately encouraged and emboldened ISIS, ISIL and Al Qaeda as well as its many Islamofascist franchises. Obviously, many mistakes were made in the 'occupation' of Iraq, but complete rapid withdrawal under a smokescreen of political rationalizations was a serious mistake. Ryan Crocker's (American Ambassador to Iraq) experience and wisdom needed to be called upon much more.

Professorial speechifying, lecturing, shaming and reasoning with ISIS or Putin will never change their behavior or reduce their threat.

Peter Olsson

Pete's Further Thoughts on Muslim Islamofascism

Larry

Of course, there are ISIS cells in all U.S. states. Muslim Islamofascism world dominating caliphate plans are right on schedule, as Turabi, Zawahiri and Bin Laden planned and announced in Khartoum, Sudan in 1991. Our current government won't even name the enemy and only sends drone strikes to stir up the hornets' nest, as if killing a few AL Qaeda, and ISIS cockroach leaders like Osama bin Laden will defeat the Muslim IslamoFascists. Our killing of Osama made him a hero martyr for countless new ISIS cell leaders. Some are coming across our southern border which our government says is secure but clearly isn't. Many American youths seem more concerned about destroying Confederate and AMERICAN flags, attacking our police and military, just when we need them.

And, as 2016 approaches, Americans seem caught between our love of freedom and free stuff and a floundering sense of personal responsibility in a wasteland of staggering national debt as well as poisonous progressivist political correctness. I am glad I am 74 today and not 34.

Peter Olsson

Larry Answers Pete

These times remind me of the "Nero-fiddles-while-Rome-burns" statement. I see the problem with Radical Islamic Terrorism being that they are everywhere in the world. I do see a serious attempt at a world-wide caliphate. It was attempted before by the Muslims in earlier times. In fact, the Christian Crusades of the 11th Century was in response to Muslim wars of expansion and an attempt to keep control of Middle East holy sites considered sacred by both Muslims and Christians.

The conflict between these two warring religions continued for centuries and as recently as the 17th Century Spain dealt harshly with the Moors and Muslims. I am not condoning any past actions on either side, but simply acknowledge that Islam and Christian countries (if any Western countries still consider themselves Christian countries) have been warring for centuries.

With this newest renewal of Islamic-Western Civilization conflict, I don't see any end in sight.

I agree with you. I am glad I am aging too, but I seriously fear for our children and grandchildren. We are not leaving them a peaceful legacy.

Larry

Pete's Considering of Obama Father-Hunger

Larry

The specific psychodynamic domain of my concern about Barack Obama is his **unresolved father-hunger** as illustrated in his book, *Dreams **From** My Father* ("**from**", not "**of**" My Father). This subtle word use by Obama is picked up on and developed by Dinesh D'Souza in his book *The Roots of Obama's Rage*. Basically, while not abused by his father, Obama was essentially neglected and abandoned by his father. Obama seems to have denied this and defensively and ambivalently idealizes his father and strong father /mentor figures as a means of psychological self –protection. They are really myths about his own self creation; in other words, Obama is in search of his father himself. True of all Pied Pipers, malignant or benign as I noted in my book, *Malignant Pied Pipers of Our Time.*

I believe that Obama's father-hunger led him to be passive and admiring in the presence of men like Tony Resko, William Ayers, Rev. Jeremiah Wright, Saul Alinsky, and his Hawaiin high school mentor the Communist, Mr. Frank Marshall Davis, and, by association, his father, Barack Sr.

Obama denounced these defective father figures only after they made their radical views obvious to "the public", or, in Resko's case, was imprisoned! Even when Obama denounced these unsavory individuals, it was accompanied by no clear explanation of how he had been duped, or why he didn't confront these men directly and proactively. Obama offered as initial explanations only vague allusions to Rev. Wright as his pastor of twenty years to whom he had loyalty. Rev. Wright baptized his daughters. Yet, Obama chose Wright's sermon title for the name of his book, *The Audacity of Hope*. John McCain and Mitt Romney were reluctant to confront these areas effectively during their TV debates with Obama.

Obama considered Ayers as just some guy in his neighborhood who did bad things when Obama was eight years old. That pronouncement seems incredibly lame coming from an intelligent law school professor and the fact that Obama's senate campaign was kicked off in Ayers' home! Also, Obama and Ayers worked together for years on the Board forming policy for an educational charity, the Annenberg Foundation. Obama also wrote a glowing review of Ayers' slanted but fascinating book, *A Kind and Just Parent*, about the Chicago Juvenile Courts. Strange how none of this was investigated by the Main Stream Media at the time.

I fear that like some subtle modern "Manchurian Candidate", Obama was influenced by Wright's Black Liberation Theology. Ayers' radical childhood indoctrination ideas masquerading as education, and that Alinsky , Frank Marshall Davis and Barack Sr. have influenced Obama greatly! Further depth of investigation of Obama by the media about these matters would have been helpful to me, and many others, as a voter. Regardless, most of us Americans have apparently been intoxicated by "The Audacity of Obama Vintage Hope".

As I asked and answered in December 2010, "How can Barack Obama's Personality be described?"

I think Obama's unique disorders of the self are best described as an "As If Personality", a

variant of what has recently been called Narcissistic Personality Disorder by psychiatrists and

psychologists..

In Barack Obama's book, *Dreams From my Father,* Obama in a very literate way uses his own search for his father as a means of trying to create his inner self. Obama builds a pedestal for his father-himself. His father couldn't cure Africa with his vintage of socialism, and Obama appears to want to cure the world via his revamping of America to fit his own grandiose, messianic and utopian self as a great leader. This appears to be operating at an unconscious level because his eloquent speeches seem idealized, optimistic and utopian in tone and content.

Larry's Brief Remarks

Very insightful thoughts, Pete. I certainly yield to your analysis based on your professional study and practice as a psychiatrist/psychoanalyst for many years. These remarks will help me grow in my understanding of what is, to me, a deeply disturbing and incompetent leader, namely Obama.

Larry

Pete and the Beer Summit

Remember the infamous "Beer Summit" when Biden and Obama smoothed over the arrest of Harvard Professor Gates by a Cambridge Policeman? Obama called Gates by his nick name "Skip" and falsely accused the Cambridge police of stupidity toward Obama's old friend?

Last night I happened to see on PBS a two hour, somewhat revisionist, rewrite of African history called "Ancient African Civilizations and leaders". It had beautiful cinematography and basically Skip Gates was the star leading a tour of archeologic excavations and interviews with African archeologists and Ivy League professors of theology, history, anthropology and archaeology. Gates was prominent in every scene from the tip of South Africa through Olduvi Gorge (Richard Leakey's discovery of the African genesis of mankind) through Kenya to the Nile river valleys up to Sudan, Egypt and over to North Africa through Gibraltar.

One major but subtle thesis of the program was that Christianity did not come to Africa from European Colonialization but started in East African in ancient areas of the Kush. In Professor Gates' opinion this was a true African Genesis and Eden.

Another theme was the equality, intermingling of primitive Christianity in East Africa and Islam. Gates implies, at times, of a historical **superiority** of Islam! The archeological structures were amazing and worth the seeing of Gate's movie. The project for the film was financed through Bank of America

My Hunch: Obama took a course of Gate's at Harvard and became friends with Gates. It would be helpful to have a copy of Obama's transcripts to prove or disprove my hunch. I think it may explain Obama's insistence that he is a Christian but also ambivalently adoring of Islam. Rev Wright may have turned Obama off so much that he began to embrace Islam and fuse his Christian identity with African, Kenyan Islam. It also touches on a connection between Obama's dislike of Churchill, Israel (**Not God's chosen people in Obama's mind**) and Obama's hatred

of Colonialization and his grandiose embrace of his vintage view of utopian Globalism!

Check out Gate's Wikipedia page---very interesting stuff. See the PBS special if you can.

Pete

Larry Responds to Pete

Thanks Pete for the tip. I will look for that special. I have always been intrigued by the study of archaeology and how it might prove the Biblical stories. Many of the Bible stories have been proven true while some remain speculation. The more we learn about our past, distant and near, the more we can understand the present.

Larry

Excerpt from One of Pete's Books that has a Bearing on this Topic

Excerpt from *Malignant Pied Pipers of our Time;* (Publish America, 2005)

Peter A. Olsson, M.D.

Pied Piper-type leaders have experienced intense disappointments in their own parents and often their home community. This occurs via neglect, abandonment, shame, or humiliation during their childhood. As the years go by, their loneliness and memories of empathy-starved, neglected and shame-dominated childhoods become magnified. It is as if these lonely, humiliating years had become an inner psychological deformity. These poignant experiences of neglect, shame, psychological abandonment and fear of being alone in a charismatic leader, lead them toward dramatic action. Actions provide a sense, however spurious, of inner restitution, triumph and even revenge. They eventually crave and need followers. The evolving dynamic in the follower group is a two-way street between the members' passive or masochistic narcissism, and the active, aggressive behavior advocated and orchestrated by the narcissistic leader. This time the leader feels empowered, rather than powerless as he had felt in childhood. The leader gains a sense of power and mastery over their own early childhood feelings of insignificance. They become overwhelmingly significant and powerful in the lives of their followers. Beneath the outward confidence and swagger of the leader is an unconscious sense of shame and a fear of humiliation ready to surface when the leader's progressively fragile narcissism is punctured.

I believe that Barack Hussein Obama is a Political Pied Piper. Malignant? YES!

Dinesh D'Souza in his book, *The Roots of Obama's Rage*, captures the key and core psychological and social psychological dynamics that consciously, pre-consciously, and unconsciously drive and motivate much of Barack Obama's personal and political behavior. These potential psychological blind spots are important since he is our president!

In clinical, social and academic situations I have observed that in the domain of personality diagnosis and psychodynamic formulations about individuals, most people take astute observations about themselves as accusations rather than potentially constructive observations. A rare individual relishes, values and makes cogent, effective, growth-promoting use of observations about their personality. I believe that Obama is too defensive to make creative use of criticism to implement inner change of himself, as opposed to external political speechifying and political maneuvering.

Obama's deferential mannerisms and peculiar grin around world leaders looks charming on the surface, as does his dramatic "Compassion" but, these lead me to speculate about the inner struggles that Obama seems to have towards power, submission and dependency. But in reality, Obama's apparent independency occurs to make him feel strong and aloof and above us plebeians.

Pete Olsson

More Comments by Pete

I used to try to understand Obama's actions, decisions and indecisions as either based on Saul Alinsky's tactics for radicals, Chicago style politics (i.e. every decision purely politically-based and to the base) or Obama's appeal to his grandiose highly idealized utopian vision of "Social Justice" as Obama conceives of it. If only Putin, even ISIS would listen to Obama's rational, appeal to an ultimately evolving benevolent **history**. I think all the previous are involved with Obama's utopian mentation, but recently he has been showing definite signs of what self-psychologists/psychoanalysts call fragmentation of the self.

To illustrate, I add the following:

Considering recent events surrounding Barack Obama's "Disengagement", dithering and indecisive decision-making around foreign policy and overly aggressive and impulsive domestic actions of "Pen and phone" (These seem like reaction formations, much like a person fearful of heights that becomes a test pilot).

I ask myself what a psychoanalytic colleague recently asked me, "Pete, Obama looks severely aged, irritable and angry. Do you think he is depressed?"

Obama certainly has suffered very active devaluing, increasingly well founded direct media criticism and psychologically painful affronts to his competence and overly inflated self-esteem. He says he wants to make careful decisions and "Not do stupid stuff" (His core foreign policy?!).

I think he just doesn't know what to do on any consistent basis!

I subsequently have asked myself two questions:

(1) **Typically, what are the symptoms when a narcissistic personality disorder gets significantly depressed?** Rather than sleep problems, self-derogation, loss of energy, loss of appetite, weight. loss, suicidal thoughts and loss of libido, the narcissistic personality typically grows more aloof, detached, arrogant, haughty,

and isolated from all those who don't bolster his self-esteem, brilliance and importance. All who challenge the narcissist are devalued, shamed and treated sardonically and with devaluing sarcastic humor. Sexuality is "Selfie-focused".

In recent times Obama relies almost exclusively on Valerie Jarret his worshipful consigliere and his worshipful VP Biden. Hollywood and wealthy Wall Street donors writing big - buck checks, and worshipful golf buddies give Obama companionship and support. To my knowledge he no longer even plays golf with John Boehner (A scratch golfer to contrast with Obama's pitiful golf swing. I seriously doubt that he works truly collaboratively with his military advisors, our allies, his UN secretary and, for sure, not with Republicans)

(2) **How does fragmentation of the self in a narcissistic character disorder affect his decision-making?**

When faced with key decisions, the narcissist, under pressure, gets more rigid, self-absorbed and preoccupied with his own image, importance and omnipotence. The group he leads increasingly is secondary to his own wishes, importance and power to overcome an increasing sense of powerlessness.

I believe that at an unconscious level, Obama is still a frightened little boy in a strange Muslim school in Indonesia and he is totally ambivalent to the core about killing any Muslim, I think folks can apply this to our fragmenting leader Barack Obama. Putin out-maneuvers

Obama at every turn because Obama's tepid narcissism is very apparent to Putin at a gut-level and is exploited.

Peter Olsson

OBAMATHINK and OBAMA GROUPTHINK

Peter Olsson

We psychoanalysts frequently observe so called "Freudian Slips" in ourselves, others, and work groups. Clear, solid leadership is crucial in a work group like the president's cabinet. (In the author's opinion, Obama rarely has effective cabinet meetings!) Ultimately, like much of his childhood, he was/ is a loner with a smiling, affable, charming surface. He is more comfortable with a room of admiring campaign workers or fawning crowds at a campaign rally, than one-on-one with an intelligent critic or group of constructive critics. He never admits or seems to learn from a mistake.

There is a corollary to so-called "Groupthink" that I call Group Unconscious Belief (GUB). GUB reflects the collective unconscious of a group. If the leader, in this case Obama, has intense ambivalence about war in general, and HIS war (Afghanistan), vs Bush's war (Iraq), in particular, then, slips, unconscious leaks, and often and particularly on Obama's part, inaction and dithering, (rationalized as 'careful study and thought) are bound to occur. Remember when Obama announced his surge in Afghanistan and at the same time he foolishly announced when our troops would be leaving? (Unconscious, or preconscious slip?)

In my opinion, Obama's core wish, desire and goal has not been solidifying victories in Iraq and Afghanistan to protect our country's interests from global fascist Islamism. Instead, he wants, the emotionally appealing goal of merely getting our troops back home PRONTO. Regardless of the consequences for our national security.

Obama's long term and, I think, wrong-headed, idealistic, lawyerly goal is a utopian world peace based on international Obama vintage lawyerly utopia. A mixture of Sharia law and Obama's mental picture of lawyerly social justice. Obama even thinks Russia, Iran and China can be won over to his professorial, philosopher-king and god-like community organized world.

Obama's lieutenants' and minions' slips, leaks, actions, regulations all backed up by Obama's pen and omnipotent speechifying head toward the God-prince's utopian goal. Can you hear John Lennon's beautiful sounding lyrics and music---IMAGINE?

And two more years to get there. Ah, but the unconscious mind is timeless.

Pete Olsson

Larry's Suspicions

My suspicions and worst fears are coming true. The uber-racist Farrakhan has now called for the elimination of the American Flag because it is racist. And in an article in today's New Hampshire Union Leader by Wayne Hester he states, "...leaders in Tennessee said a bust of Nathan Bedford Forrest, a Confederate general and Ku Klux Klan's first grand wizard, should be removed from the State House...In New Orleans, pressure is growing to remove a monument of Jefferson Davis, a slave owner who led the Confederate States of America during the Civil War... Also, in New Orleans Mayor Mitch Landrieu called for the removal of a 60-foot statue of Robert E. Lee, Commander of the Confederate Army of Northern Virginia. . California State Assemblywoman, Lorena Gonzalez, a Democrat, urged the San Diego Unified School District to rename an elementary school named after Lee. Anyone associated with the Confederate Army, she said, is linked to intolerance and racism.... In Kentucky, calls were also growing to remove a Davis statue. 'The Jefferson Davis statue belongs in a museum, where history is taught, rather than in the State Capitol where laws are made said Kentucky state Attorney General Jack Conway."

And so, as you can see, the ball has just begun to roll. If all vestiges of slavery must be abolished and destroyed, we will begin to look like ISIS which destroys all vestiges of a religious past as they blow up statues and monuments in Iraq and Syria. Shall we rename all schools, streets, towns with any hint of the Confederacy in their names? Shall all history books be rewritten to purge them of all things Confederate? Shall we purge our history of any KKK member in Congress? If so, Democrat Senator Robert Byrd of Virginia, is, to use a pun, history. He was a recruiter for his local KKK and rose to the title of Kleagle and Exalted Cyclops. I guess that made him special, as far as the KKK is concerned.

Be careful America. Be very careful. The hypocrisy entwined in this rush to appear "on the right side of history" is palpable. For example, Walmart CEO, Douglas McMillon told Fox Business, "We don't want any of the merchandise we sell to be offensive." Really? REALLY??? Walmart "...sells posters of Argentine revolutionary Che Guevara, who personally presided over firing squads and established Cuba's labor camps, where dissidents, poets, gays and other enemies of the state are held as slaves." Although I cannot recall where I read this I agree with its content. In a recent article it stated, "Because American History is replete with contradictions, we purge at our peril."

History must be understood in its context. What was once considered "right" may not be now. But to attempt to erase our history is to lose all touch with it and **its lessons**. While it is trite to quote Santana, he is right. Those who forget the past are condemned to repeat it. Well, America, we are not just forgetting it, we are purposely now erasing all vestiges of it. I predict a push back or backlash. While many flag makers will cease making any more Confederate flags, I suspect at least one will, or one will now start up to produce them and many people, Northerners and Southerners alike will start flying them everywhere. Not as a statement of racism, but as a statement of freedom of expression and regional and historical pride. Personally, I could no more fly a Confederate flag than I could fly the Nazi Swastika, but as Voltaire said, "I do not agree with what you have to say, but I'll defend to the death your right to say it."

The slope is getting very slippery. Has any country or culture existed without some blame or shame in its past? Virtually all societies have practiced the atrocious act of slavery. Many still do, but America absolutely does not. While there may be people who are racist, there is no institutional racism in America. Why not recognize our great strides in this area as well? It seems to be endemic in human nature to some extent. But in America we fought our most bloody war, partly to stamp slavery out. Why is that not mentioned? America may be flawed in some ways, but at least we attempt to correct our faults. If we are such a bad nation, why is America still sought after by so many refugees? Certainly, Europe is now awash in African refugees fleeing Africa, but they go there because it is close by. Many Europeans, Africans and others from around the world endure horrible sacrifice to seek out this wonderful country where freedom still exists, at least for now.

I pray daily for our healing. We need a solid Conservative President to lead us back to God and patriotism. Bobby Jindal, at yesterday's announcement for running for president, was wonderful. The field is fraught with great Americans on the Republican side and consists of Socialists on the left. The choice could not be starker. November 2016 will tell all of us where America is going.

God bless America.

Larry

Pete Answers

SPOT-ON LARRY!

Pete Publishes Some Important Questions

Published in ACADEMY FORUM (of the American Academy of Psychoanalysis and Dynamic Psychiatry) OPINION--Vol. 57 No.1, Spring 2013 pp.25-28.

A PSYCHIATRIST-PSYCHOANALYST ASKS BARACK OBAMA

SIX PERSONAL MENTAL HEALTH QUESTIONS

Peter A. Olsson MD

(*) Indicate reference to the glossary.

Dear President Obama:

You seem reluctant to make creative use of criticism. Rather than implementing positive inner changes as derived from constructive criticism and reaching effective compromises in your policies, you repeatedly project (*1) blame via speechifying and verbally attacking your critics. This is so even when the criticisms seem cogent and respectful. Your defensiveness seems brittle even fragile, and incompatible with your abilities and talents as reflected in your memoir.

The Wonder and Magic Charm of Words

We psychoanalysts view speech acquisition as a decisive step in the foundation of the executive domain of the human mind. In our early childhood, speech is experienced as a magic charm. It is directed toward forcing the external world and fate to do those things that have been conjured up in our words. David Maraniss in his book about you, describes your comment in the English class of Ms. Czurles-Nelson at Punahou School as the class discussed what people fear the most. You said,

> "WORDS...words are the power to be feared most...whether directed personally or internationally, words can be weapons of destruction." (Maraniss.)

Mr. Obama, our childhood words continue to be important later as adults, even when the early omnipotent magic is gradually tempered by reality. Your speeches at home and abroad seem to ring with a magic charm and charisma. They allude to majestic collective ideals, even utopianism.

Mr. Obama, this essay will use your 1995 book, *Dreams From My Father: A Story of Race and Inheritance*, and your media comments and behavior as a basis for asking you six key personal mental health questions.

Sally Jacob's carefully documented book, *The Other Barack: The Bold and Reckless*, provides further information about your father... Barak Obama Sr. Several key questions I present will relate to your poignant descriptions of your mother, your grandmother(s), and various siblings.

QUESTION#1—How do you understand your identification (*2) with your father and the implications this has for the stability of your narcissism and self-confidence. What are the implications of this question for your leadership and ability to govern?

It is a psychological truism that fathers are important to our personality formation. We all have internal representation of our parents' personalities, their authority; their love of us... or lack of it. For better or worse, we embrace or rebel against our inner parents. Denial of our parents' influence, or, blind idealizing or devaluing of them, has profound consequences for our emotional life and trajectory of our maturation.

Mr. Obama, your book *DREAMS FROM MY FATHER,* has a lyrical searching style. You convey a Billy Budd tone of innocent inquiry that is touching and moving. Your writing is bold and courageous in its self-disclosure and creative curiosity. You and your Kenyan relatives frequently call your father "The Old Man". The candor and eloquence of your memoir seems to reflect an intertwining of your genuine search for your father, and simultaneously for your true self. Your poignant words about the "island of your grandfather Onyango's shame" and Barak Obama Sr's quest for power and recognition leap from the pages of your memoir when you say,

"He (Barak Sr.) had almost succeeded, in a way his own father (Onyango) could never have hoped for. And then, after seeming to travel so far, to discover that he had not escaped at all! To discover that he remained trapped on his father's island, with its fissures of anger and doubt and defeat, the emotions still visible beneath the surface, hot and molten and alive, like a wicked, yawning mouth, and his mother gone, gone, away..." (pp 428-429).

Your vivid "yawning mouth" metaphor resounds with implications of what we psychoanalysts understand about the concepts of psychological introjections (*3) and incorporation (*3) ... and the notion of oral aggression (*3).

Mr. Obama, your island metaphor seems to accurately fit Onyango, Barak, and yourself... and all three of your maternal/parental introjects (*3), (See (*9) deposits. (Many islands here...Hawaii... a huge one, Kenya a metaphorical one, and the haunting inner "island of silence" that best be overcome... because as you aptly imply...no Obama man ultimately is an island.) After describing your inner thoughts and emotions you seek further closure with these powerful words,

"For a long time, I sat between the two graves and wept. When my tears were spent, I felt a calmness wash over me. I felt the circle finally close. I realized that who I was, what I cared about, was no longer just a matter of intellect or obligation, no longer a construct of words. I saw that my life in America—the black life, the white life, the sense of abandonment I'd felt as a boy, the frustration and hope I'd witnessed in Chicago—all of it related to this small plot of earth an ocean away, connected by more than the accident of a name or the color of my skin. The pain I felt was my father's pain. My questions were my brothers' questions. Their struggle, my birthright." (pp 429-430).

This scene you describe is intense, poignant...and even a sacred sounding epiphany experience.

The narrative that emerges from your remarkable dialogue with your relatives and your own intensely personal peregrinations, reminds me of the narrative that emerges during my work as a psychotherapist with highly intelligent and well-motivated patients. A key difference between your search for your father-yourself via your process of memoir writing and a depth psychotherapy experience however, is the absence of a therapist. A therapist to confront you with your psychological blind-spots and to support you in applying and extending your insights about your father/yourself. Such consolidating psychotherapeutic help would reduce the propensity for excessive chameleon-like trends in your personality.

Your father was clearly a highly intelligent man but had a difficult and conflicted relationship with his own father... your grandfather Hussein Onyango. Your Granny told you, "Even from the time he (Onyango) was a boy, your grandfather was strange. It is said of him that he had ants up his anus, because he could not sit still". Granny goes on, "He was very serious always—he never laughed or played games with the other children, and never made jokes." (p379). (You Mr. Obama, like your vice president, seem to have a lively, even aggressive sense of humor. You enjoy jokes, playing golf, and being playful with your children. This indicates strength. Freud once told a journalist when asked how a person might be happy..." a person must learn to work and love" ...I would add, "and to play".) At times Mr. Obama, you seem to play too much and govern and lead too little. Your speechifying seems to be one of your favorite ways to play.

In addition, Onyango, like you and your father Barak, seem(s) to have a keen sense of curiosity and eagerness to learn... even from "the white man".

QUESTION #2—In your moving memoir you are candid about the white vs. black struggle within yourself. You seem to entwine this issue with your search for your roots of identity in Kenya. You also show great empathy for blacks and minorities who have been abused by white slave traders, white colonialists, and white oppressors... even some within the American political system. However, are you able to accurately perceive, collaborate with, and compromise with older white Republican politician colleagues who vigorously oppose your policies and philosophy? Do you think such white men stir transferences (*4) within your mind? Your unresolved transferences likely create subconscious re-enactments (*5) of your father, mother and grandfather/yourself, which in turn can result in stubborn political stalemates with powerful white Republicans.

When unconscious identifications, introjections and transferences gain ascendancy in strong emotional contexts, destructive acting-out***** is possible. Or inaction! During crucial political decision-making and compromise, the most freedom from unconscious conflict is the ideal. However, it is easier said than done... as you well know. You seem to have a healthy rapport with Joe Biden (positive transference) who even shares your father's trait of verbal aggressiveness, sometimes inappropriate in its extent. It obviously could be more difficult with white Republicans such as Romney, Graham, O'Connell, Kyle, Ryan, Cantor or McCain. You seem curt, abrupt and dismissive, with these white guys. It seemed less conflicted for you with John Boehner on the golf course and you two were very close to a creative compromise.

Question #3—What are your ideas and intuitions about the roots of your father's relentless ambition, severe alcoholism, pathological lying, obsessive philandering, and significant character defects?

Mr. Obama, you said, "My image of Onyango, faint as it was, had always been of an autocratic man—a cruel man, perhaps. But I had also imagined him an independent man, a man of his people, opposed to white rule. There is no real basis for this image I now realized—only the letter he had written to Gramps, (Your maternal grandfather in Hawaii), saying that he didn't want his son marrying white." (p406). According to Jacobs, Onyango was alienated from his own father for most of the eighty years of his life.

From your reports from your Kenyan relatives and Sally Jacob's research, I conclude that Onyango who was called "The Terror" by many family members, was very accomplished but harsh, domineering, and obsessively controlling. He seemed to express perpetual disappointment toward your father, Barak Sr. Interesting to me is that your father Barak Sr. wrote books he called *OTIENO* ("The Wise Man").

Also, profoundly significant is your father's early loss of his mother through abandonment. You experienced traumatic separations from your mother whose troubled relationships with your father and stepfather led to painful disruptions and dislocations for you. Psychodynamic psychiatrists would connect your father's maternal loss as a causal factor in your father's severe addiction to alcohol, his obsessive philandering, and character defects; including many episodes of pathologic lying. My intuition is that your father harbored enormous unconscious anger toward his father, his mother, and all authority figures. His unconscious mind was not user friendly toward women though he charmed many. He eventually demanded feeding, nurturing, and affection from all the women he successfully seduced or romanced. If his white wife Ruth didn't feed him as he demanded, he verbally abused her (Oral aggression (*3) and beat her and her children. Like father Onyango... like son, Barak Sr.

Your father's biographer Sally Jacobs states,

"" When Obama (Sr.) headed to America he left behind a pregnant wife and a young son, all of whom seemed to vanish into the parched red dust of Kenya. He neither spoke of them nor acknowledged them to school or immigration officials until, that is, he deemed them an asset to his resume...In America he would marry one white woman, propose to another and seduce many more.

Polygamy was surely an aspect of his culture but in the Luo tradition a husband makes his home with all his wives. Obama Sr. did just the opposite: moving from one to the next and betraying each woman and the children he didn't father (psychologically)."

A sad but true summary.

QUESTION #4—Do you think your father's relentless academic and political ambition was related to his unconscious and desperate wish to gain his father's approval? Did your father's narcissistic hurt and resulting rage cause rigid reflex anger at all authority?

In your book you said that your father was on the African student airlift to the USA. According to Jacobs, Obama Sr. was rejected for that student airlift by Robert F. Stephens chief of USIO. Stephen's did not like your father because he was "Cocksure, far more confident than his resume deserved."

It was eventually a white woman benefactor named Ms. Mooney who pulled strings and helped finance Barak Sr.'s ticket to education in America.

As you learned from your family in Kenya, your father from his early school years onward behaved like a know-it-all. He would correct and defy his teachers in front of the class. You report, "His teacher would scold Barak for his insolence, but Barak would refuse to back down. "(p415).

Jacobs reports that a friend of your father named Abercrombie, said, "He was a very daunting personality...He just couldn't contain his irritation with people who were not as facile as he." Even at Harvard your father so offended some professors and administrators that it leads to his PHD never being completed.

Your father's relentless, impulsive and cocky know-it-all attitude led to his downfall. He asserted himself as if he were the perpetual and ultimate authority speaking truth to power. When this combined with his ever-progressive drinking, pathological lying and defiance---he ended up in abject poverty and showed suicidal behaviors while driving.

QUESTION#5—Do you note within yourself an identification or introjection of your father's verbal style...i.e. a stubborn, impulsive, cocky urge to assert verbal power when feeling on the extemporaneous spot? Does this verbal impulsiveness seem automatic?... difficult to resist? I hypothesize that in addition to identification and introjection, you show signs of agendas your father, mother and grandparents unconsciously **deposited (*9)** in you. "Memories belonging to one person cannot be transmitted to another person. However, an adult may "deposit" his or her own injured self-images within a child along with images of others— even sometimes the image of perpetrators or persecutors. In depositing, the adult actively plants his or her specific images into the developing self-representation of the. The adult thus uses the child unconsciously as a permanent reservoir for certain self-and other images belonging to that adult. These mental images and agendas are pushed into the child, without the experimental/contextual framework that created them." In my opinion, your mother, father and grandparents pushed deposits of their unresolved anger, fear and grandiose desire to rescue the world from the racism and victimization in life they felt. You appear to project these agendas on to your perpetual campaign of rescuing America.

Examples of your unconscious acting –out (*6), your part in the precipitation of the infamous "Beer Summit" highlights your Ready-Fire-Aim verbal impulsiveness. When asked about the alleged police misconduct in Cambridge at the tail end of your press conference, you at first said that we needed to await the results of the full investigation of the event before reaching conclusions. Then suddenly in the next impulsive breath you said that the white Cambridge police were stupid! Not your verbally aggressive black Harvard professor friend.

On another occasion you impulsively defended Eric Holder's half-cocked idea of trying KSM and other Islamist killers in down - town Manhattan. You said Americans shouldn't worry, the 9/11 killers would be executed eventually anyway. Your comments could have been used by a clever Jihadi or U.S. lawyer to demand a mistrial because of your influence on a jury pool.

A third example occurred at the very start of your presidency when you starkly stated that GITMO would be closed within one year. Then, you studied the situation and now after several years GITMO has been expanded. The world clearly realizes that though imperfect, GITMO is run humanely, and the prisoners are treated better and more justly than in their home countries. You and AG Holder still seem ambivalent about GITMO to this day.

Your charisma and powerfully effective oratorical skill is impressive and serves the leadership of America best when it is as free as possible ...of your unresolved unconscious conflicts being acted-out (*6).

Mr. Obama, your ego strengths are many. Clearly, you have successfully triumphed over your earlier substance abuse...even cigarettes. Your marital relationship seems to show a commitment to intimacy, communication and loving approaches to marriage and parenting of your beloved daughters. This clearly represents transcendence of the insecure and pathetic lack of collaborative intimacy exampled in your father's life and behavior. Your efforts to form a healthy identity in this regard, seems to have been very successful. The famous psychoanalyst Erik Erikson called this domain *Basic Trust*. Early childhood separations, losses and neglect makes this no mean a task.

QUESTION#6—Finally Mr. Obama, if your father was one of your top economic advisors today, what major directions would he recommend for our US Economy? How much does his thinking impact on your preconscious (*7) and unconscious (*8) mind?

In your father's July 1965 paper in the East Africa Journal entitled "PROBLEMS FACING OUR SOCIALISM", his economic and political philosophy more than peeks through as your father speaks about land reform,

> "Would it not seem, then, that the government could bring more rapid consolidation through clan cooperatives? Individual initiative is not usually the best method of bringing land reform." (p29.)

Barak goes on about "society" or the ultra-collective in general,

> "If one were to suppose that the state is an instrument of society and if the society regards growth as well as the correction of the lopsided development … (? rich vs poor majority) … which has characterized this country as important, then, the society, through the government which is its instrument, should enforce means by which this growth and change can be brought about." (p29).

In the next paragraph he says about "class problems',

> "But we also need to eliminate power structures that have been built through excessive accumulation so that only a few individuals shall control a vast magnitude of resources as is the case now." (p29).

Mr. Barack Obama II, this rigidly repetitive theme appears in a lot of your speeches. Finally, Barak Sr. says about TAXATION on P30,

> "Certainly, there is no limit to taxation if the benefits derived from public services by society measure up to the cost in taxation which they have to pay. It is a fallacy to say there is this limit and it is a fallacy to rely mainly on individual free enterprise to get the savings." (p30).

Three sentences later Barak Sr. says,

"Yet one who has read Marx cannot fail to see that corporations are not only what Marx referred to as the advanced stage of capitalism, but Marx even called it finance capitalism by which a few would control the finances of so many and through this have not only economic power but political power as well." (p30).

Mr. Obama, you in speeches have scoffed at people who have raised the question about your possible Neo-Marxist or Sol Alinsky vintage thinking... or that of your entourage. But, it seems important that you have a clear conscious awareness of your father's Neo-Marxism as stated above. Conscious awareness of your thinking in contrast to that of "The Other Barack" is important as the election campaign proceeds this year. You vigorously deny any conscious efforts to divide America via class warfare or black vs. white, but, at times your words and those of your attorney general raise questions. At a conscious level I do not impute your motives.

This essay is presented candidly and respectfully and with my conscious awareness that you are not my patient and my profession's ethics descry any psychiatrist that comments about someone they have not personally examined. I chose to do this anyway, because of the magnitude of the issues facing our country. I also admire the candor of your memoir and I attempt the same in my questions.

*GLOSSARY:

(1)   Projection: A defense mechanism, operating **unconsciously,** in which what is emotionally unacceptable in the self is unconsciously rejected and attributed (projected) to others.

(2)   Identification: A defense mechanism, operating unconsciously, by which one patterns oneself after some other person. Identification plays a major role in the development of one's personality and specifically of the superego. To be differentiated from imitation or role modeling which is a conscious process.

(3) Introjection: A defense mechanism, operating unconsciously whereby loved or hated external objects are symbolically absorbed within oneself. The converse of projection. It may serve as a defense against conscious recognition of intolerable hostile impulses. This mechanism is related to the more primitive FANTASY of oral **incorporation and oral aggression. Also, see (9) Deposit.**

(4) Transference: The unconscious assignment to others of feelings and attitudes that were originally associated with important figures (parents, siblings, grandparents, etc.) in one's early life. The psychiatrist or therapist. utilizes this phenomenon as a therapeutic tool to help the patient understand emotional problems, their origins and resolution.

(5) Enactment/Re-enactment: In the context of a trusting and effective therapeutic relationshipactual reactivation of childhood experiences may occur like a flashback in a movie. Without the containment of a therapeutic alliance, destructive acting-out***** may occur.

(6) Acting-Out: Expressions of unconscious emotional conflicts or feelings in actions rather than words...or words that are ill-chosen because the person is not consciously aware of the meaning of the words or actions.

(7) Preconscious: Thoughts that are not in immediate awareness but that can be recalled by conscious effort.

(8) Unconscious: That part of the mind or mental functioning of which the content is only rarely subject to awareness. It is a repository for data that has never been conscious or that may have been conscious and later repressed.

(9) Deposit: An adult person unconsciously uses a child as a permanent reservoir for certain self- and other painful images belonging to that adult. The experiences that created these painful mental images in the adult are not accessible to the child. Yet, those mental images are pushed into the child, without the experiential/contextual framework which originally created them. Much less... an explanatory cognitive process to deal with the deposited images or behavioral imperatives. (Volkan,V. (2013" Karnac Publishing, London.

REFERENCES:

American Psychiatric Glossary. Seventh Edition. APPI Press 1994.

Obama, Barack (1995). DREAMS FROM MY FATHER. Three Rivers Press,

New York.

Jacobs, Sally (2011) THE OTHER BARAK: The Bold and Reckless Life of

President Barack Obama's Father

Obama, Barak H. (July, 1965). "Problems Facing Our Socialism". (Another

Critique of Session Paper No. 10). East Africa Journal pp 26-33.

Volkan, V. *Animal Killer: Transmission of War Trauma from One Generation to the Next.* Karnac Books (2013) London p7.

IMMIGRATION REFORM, OBAMAHOOD'S STYLE

Obama's illegal executive action plan to "reform" immigration laws in America--- is purely an application of his mentor Saul Alinsky's 'rules for radicals'.(see attached)

Step 1. Ask congress for action.

Step 2. Get Harry Reid to table the house bill on immigration without a vote (Obama veto not even necessary).

Step 3. Issue a Presidential Proclamation that children of illegal immigrants will not be prosecuted or deported

Step 4. When thousands and thousands of pitiful, diseased, parentless children and teenagers give themselves up on our border, first say they will be deported and then take that action back! Step 5. Request Congress, who you never worked with and insulted and mocked, for billions to take care of the poor alien children.

Step 6. When congress won't appropriate the money, shame Congress as cold-hearted and uncaring, especially your enemy, Republicans.

Step 7. Use up Immigration Customs Enforcement and Border agents' time to change diapers and baby sit the kids, so they can't patrol the border, as the kid's relatives and parents sneak across.

Step 8. Shame and stir up anger, fear and anxiety in American citizens in the communities where the kids are dumped. (These tactics further divide all Americans into the haves and have nots. Maybe even resulting in street crimes and riots!!!).

Such tactics also deflect from the VA scandal, The IRS scandal, the Benghazi Bloodgate and the mushrooming danger of Al Qaeda and its affiliates, not to mention the wars in Afghanistan and Iraq where Obama has now snatched defeat out of the jaws of fledgling victories.

Never waste a good Chicago style manufactured crisis!

Saul Alinsky is dancing a jig with Frank Marshal Davis and Barack Obama Senior in HELL.

Pete Olsson

Pete Writes to Larry on a Thomas Sowell Article

Thanks Larry for sending me the wonderful and thoughtful essay by Sowells. It counters Barack Obama's barely contained anger toward wealthy white America. "White Power", "White Advantage" and alleged "White Micro-aggressions" towards minorities are propounded by some Obama minions and elite leftist white-guilt academics. Obama seems to see himself as a Nelson Mandella figure that will shame, blame and guilt-provoke America into a reconciliation process like was accomplished in South Africa.

(Obama even tried to brag yesterday that his wonderful 'deal' with Iran was a messianic step to move America and Iran beyond decades of hostile interaction. What hooey baloney! The Iranians laugh at Obama's folly and insult him and America at the same time as we are giving them billions in THE DEAL.)

As I have said before, I think Obama has not successfully resolved his inner mulatto self (Rage at his WHITE mother for stresses she brought to his childhood by many separations, geographical moves and her checkered unsuccessful relationships with men i.e. his father figures. Obama's unresolved subconscious rage at his BLACK abandoning, alcoholic, lying, misogynistic father accounts for the other half of his hate which he seems to project on to America. His surrogate father figure in Hawaii, Frank Marshal Davis was a former head of the communist party in America! Obama's idol, Saul Alinsky combines with Davis to account for many of Obama's political tactics and Socialist ideas.

God help our grandchildren and great grandchildren if Americans don't wake up.

Pete

Larry's Comments Regarding Obama and his Leadership Concerning Iran Deal

I never thought I would see the day when our own president was our worst enemy. Even dictators abroad are not as dangerous as a rogue, hate-filled president wielding unlimited power with the Republican opposition in disarray and cowardly sitting on their hands. I don't know what power Obama has over our Conservatives, but they all talk but do nothing meaningful. Even if both the Senate and House vote to cancel this capitulation agreement, Obama will veto it and we won't have enough votes to override his veto. It would only take two nukes to wipe out Israel completely. One on Tel Aviv and the other on Jerusalem. I visited Israel for 10 days and went everywhere north and south, east and west. Tel Aviv, Jerusalem, Masada, Sea of Galilee and Dead Sea. Stayed in a Kibbutz in the desert near Gaza. The country is beautiful and prosperous, but, geographically, it is minute. It is simply not large enough to sustain a nuclear bomb or two. And with Obama, the America hating Muslim giving Iran the bomb, it could now happen.

Ten years in the contextual time span of history is but a blink of the eye. It will be gone overnight. Think back to where you were and what you were doing 10 years ago. How fast did the time go since then? That is how fast it will be before Iran can legitimately develop a bomb with Obama's/Kerry's blessing. Kerry is no friend of America either. He fabricated his own legacy in Vietnam with his swift boat lies and then came home and threw his medals over the WH fence (that was a lie too as they weren't even his own medals. He threw someone else's medals over the fence.).

So, the world now must endure the travesty wrought upon all of us by these two traitors. Jane Fonda is gloating while thousands of American veterans and millions of right thinking Americans and Israelis are beginning to dread the future. Over the past few weeks one decision after another has gone against our conservative beliefs and Americas history of traditions. Between the Supremes and Obama/Kerry, America is now headed down a path that we may not be able to deviate from.

As for me, I am clinging to my gun and religion, even though I can't find a religion to cling to. My Lutheran church has turned secular progressive and now the Pope has done likewise so I probably won't be attending the RC church with Dolores very much anymore. Episcopalian's are way too far left and so many other Protestant sects are too secular. I am left to worship God in my own quiet, personal way. It is getting tougher and tougher to be a Christian, but then, Christ predicted this. I may just have to be content to remain faithful and wait for my demise to find some real peace again....sad. Until then I'll continue to fight what is becoming, increasingly, a more uphill battle every day.

Stay strong fellow conservatives and loyal American patriots. Go Walker/Rubio.

Larry

Larry's Further Thoughts on Obama and Kerry

I was reading this morning how Kerry is trying to convince the congress of the merits of this deal. And it struck me that it is already too late to do anything substantial. Should congress nix this deal and we don't go along with the Obama/Kerry surrender to Iran, what will happen? I seriously doubt that the rest of the world will come together to re-impose sanctions on Iran. And I wonder if even we would re-impose sanctions with this weak traitor in the WH. So, Iran will be left with nothing but time on their hands to build the nuke and the Republicans will get all the blame by Obama, Kerry and the media. They will say that the Republicans scuttled all chances for stopping Iran, even though Iran has not even been slowed down in their rush to build a nuclear bomb or missiles to deliver them. The time to stop Iran has passed. It was when all the nations, including us, had instituted sanctions. To continue them was easier than it will be now to re-impose them. So, the moment in history to really stop Iran from building a nuke is gone. And Obama/Kerry lost it to the detriment of all the world.

At this point in time, I see no real solution. Perhaps we will still exist in 2016, but as I see the cards now being played, Trump will continue to bluster, and even though I reject his style, his message is resonating with many Americans. So, if the Republicans dismiss him, I fear he will give us a Ross Perot retake. He has already dropped out of the Voters First debate here in NH which is also being simulcast in SC and Iowa because of a sarcastic editorial in the Manchester Union Leader, one of the sponsors of the debate. Consequently, he is already being alienated from the Republicans, many of whom are criticizing him quite harshly. The rift between Trump and the Republicans will only grow until he decides to run as an Independent. That will give the presidency to Hillary. God help us all when she gets elected.

So, these two events, the completion of the Iranian surrender and the election of Hillary because of Trump, will converge in 2016 with devastating consequences for all of us. I really don't see any other future currently.

Our only real hope is for Trump to not become an independent candidate, but his ego won't permit that especially since he now sees how popular he is.

Larry

Pete Writes to Larry

Larry

After watching Rubio take on Kerry today about the Iran treaty---I wrote this

DIPLOMACY AND NEGOTIATING WITH U.S. ENEMIES

Peter A. Olsson

I have always advocated negotiating even with the most dangerous and treacherous of our enemies. Formal diplomacy is valuable. Informal diplomacy also has great value.

In essence, when negotiating with treacherous and untrustworthy enemies we must be strong psychologically and appropriately suspicious. Learning about the enemy during the negotiations is as important as a signed agreement. During recent negotiations by John Kerry with Iran, it is impossible to ignore on-going calls for death to America and Israel by the ruling mullah and many of his citizens in the daily backdrop of the negotiations. Also, a concern is that Iran has not complied with its previous promises at agreements. In addition, scholars have pointed out that Islamist beliefs allow that any lie is permitted when dealing with infidels. This is called **Taqiyya** or lying to non-believers in order to draw out their vulnerability and defeat them. So, an Iranian diplomat can talk and agree in good enough faith, but his ruling Mullah(s) can cancel that in a heartbeat.

A corollary of Reagan's "Trust but verify" is, "Agree astutely and verify clearly and firmly". As Sun Tsu said long ago, and to paraphrase, If one knows fully about oneself, one will win half the battles, if one knows one's enemy as well as oneself, one will win most all battles.

The process of negotiating with treacherous enemies like Iran and North Korea always requires a quiet sense of the presence Teddy Roosevelt's big stick. Military options are not on some metaphorical table, but an element in the negotiations. No red lines broken allowed! Tactical strikes, even tactical nuclear attacks if sanctions are violated can be mentioned at the table. Embargoes, bombing attacks after increased sanctions do not imply all-out war. In fact, one current big advantage the US and free world has is that at this moment Iran, unlike the Soviets during the Cuban missile crisis, is not a nuclear power YET. And, until they would get the money from lifted sanctions they so desire, they are not able to stand up to US YET.

A completely understandable goal and narcissistic investment of a negotiator is to heroically reach an agreement. However, the most important goal is not exclusively or even necessarily an agreement, especially not at any price. In a paradoxical way, a strong negotiator must be prepared to walk away from the table several times or indefinitely. As important as an agreement reached with the enemy, is the firm clear communication of U.S. requirements, demands, values , and action consequences behind the goals of the negotiation and its success or failure.

Alexander Hamilton said, "The representatives of the people, in a popular assembly, seem sometimes to fancy that they are the people themselves, and betray strong symptoms of impatience and disgust at the least sign of opposition from any other quarter..."

(Federalist paper no. 71).

The Swiss cheese fabric of the Obama/Kerry 'deal' and the administrations bullying efforts to force it through is absurd. Even more so was Obama's pitiful, shallow and shaming-blaming performance on the Jon Daily show. Obama clearly has not spent time seriously listening to serious proposals by Rubio or Menendez . Obama's red-line dissolving, and other weaknesses has created an atmosphere that is a self-fulfilling prophesy. "The rest of the world" as Kerry calls it, won't stand with us for any so-called "Snap-back sanctions" in the future because they already sensed Obama's weakness for years.

Peter Olsson

More from Pete

It is profoundly sad and enraging to hear Obama and the smug leftist Democrats constantly ridicule George Bush and Dick Chaney. Obama's lack of class and dignity on the uber-smug/shallow Jon Daily show the other evening was beyond disgusting though Saul Alinsky would be proud. Because Obama has had few good ideas and little success in his presidency, he only can resort to blaming, shaming and devaluing his critics and the congress toward whom we pay him to provide collaborative leadership. Obama gives meager lip service to bipartisanship and then quickly asserts his haughty narcissistic defenses and projections. Me thinks the man projectith too much.

I will never forget when he invited Paul Ryan to his talk about medical care and 'entitlements'. Obama had praised Ryan's bipartisan efforts---then with pettiness put-down Ryan in that forum where Ryan could not retort. What a small man is Obama despite being 6'3".

Pete Olsson

And More

Larry, I wanted to share the e-mail I sent to my senator about the Iran deal. She always supports Obama whatever he does and only gives me polite banalities. Please write your reps and use your influence to stop this bad deal and suggest a better stronger one. I think the bottom line is that Obama/Kerry's weak negotiations and leadership led to weaknesses around the agreement over a year ago. That is why Obama says that our "partners" are dropping the sanctions soon. They want to get Iran's oil, business and sell weapons to Iran (Russia) and those weapons will eventually be used on Israel AND US

Pete Olsson

Pete's Letter to Senator Shaheen

Dear Senator, Shaheen

I was stunned by your message to me about the ill-fated Kerry/Obama 'agreement' with Iran. (1) Why did Obama /Kerry send the agreement to the UN first, before our American peoples' representatives even duly considered this dubious agreement? (Remember that Iran has never cooperated with the UN inspectors previously!)

(2) The likelihood that Russia, China, Germany, France et.al. will agree to or cooperate with the "Snap -back" of sanctions when Iran violates the agreement is zero. Mr. Obama is weak as perceived by Iran, Russia, France, Germany, China and France who all doubt Obama's leadership (I doubt his leadership in general)

(3) The tepid letter you senators sent to Iran about our hostages is pathetic in its timing! After the fact at this point..

(4) Mr. Obama has not consulted to my knowledge with Republicans like Condi Rice, Henry Kissinger, Donald Rumsfeld or Jim Baker. These people have had important points of view I am sure.

(5) Senator--please don't let Mr. Obama's arrogant, Republican and Netanyahu-bashing legacy sway your judgment about this bad deal. A much better one could have been done or still can be. Sincerely Alarmed

Peter Olsson MD

Pete's Email to Larry with Further Talks about Iran Deal

Larry, please read the agreement now that it is finally available. Kerry himself only recently saw some of the UN documents!

The more I see Kerry, Moniz and now Nicholas Burns this Am on FOX defending Obama's deeply flawed deal with Iran, the angrier and more scared I get. Here is the sequence I note.

(1) Congress and Obama have so sequestered and weakened our military that it has set us up as weak vis-a-vis Iran and THE ENTIRE WORLD.

(2) That weak leadership undermined our coalition-building against Iran prior to talks.(China, Russia, Germany and France) have cooperated with Obama on the surface but from the get go I believe they have laughed at Obama.

(3) By going around congress (Our Reps-even if they are bumblers), Obama castrated congress and US!

(4) Then in the negotiations Kerry has given up far too much and Iran has given NADA but promises. (They never keep their agreements with the West because the Koran OKs lies to infidel enemies!)

(5) The UN has never dealt effectively with Iran over nuclear inspections in the past. Why Now? By going to the UN before consulting congress and seriously listening to Israel's Intel data-- Obama asserts his utopian globalism and America's diminishment. His legacy trumps all other considerations.

(6) Nicholas Burns, on FOX today, says we need to give more money to the UN (UN=Useless Noise most of the time as Jesse Helms used to say and their wimp inspectors will have to get all of the coalitions permission and Iran's before they even can do an inspection!

And then only after 28 days!

(7) Iran now says it will not allow any US or Canadians to be on the inspection teams!

(8) The UN accepted the bogus deal with a quick unanimous vote without any thorough discussion!

(9) Kerry withdrew the conventional weapons ban demand in the 'treaty'. That means ICBMs folks.

(10) Lifting all sanctions which is Iran's main reason to even talk will free-up millions and millions to be spent on their terror enterprises against Israel and USA eventually.

(11) I predict that if an agreement is signed Israel will attack Iran's nuclear facilities with or without US. Obama will dither and speechify.

Please read this one-sided loser agreement and use your time to write to your representatives and talk with friends about the implications of rushing into this agreement now.

Peter Olsson

Pete's Email to Larry

Larry

What the article in WAPO doesn't address is specifically what Obama, as the first Mulatto US president, has personally done, not done and said, that has inflamed racial tensions in America. For example:

(1) As in the case of Professor Gates, Obama's friend, when Obama prematurely (I say impulsively) takes a side saying "The

Cambridge Mass Police were stupid". Obama just couldn't resist the jibe!

(2) Obama personalizes and, therefore, polarizes race related events such as his comment that "Travone Martin could look like my son" etc. Zimmerman, while a jerk, was found innocent.

(3) Obama is quick to send Holder, his Attorney General, to investigate the Ferguson situation to imply that there were huge race issues involved. .

(4)Holder also gave a pass to the New Black Panthers who were spewing hate speech about whites and intimidating people at the polls. Neither Obama nor Holder spoke much about the officer being innocent to balance out some other bad police racisms.

(5) When a white woman gets shot and killed in San Francisco by an illegal alien felon who had been sheltered by Obama's Pen and Phone actions (supporting Sanctuary City policies) Obama never even called the woman's family, much less offering to speak at her funeral.

(6) When the black mayor and city attorney in Baltimore aggravated the riot situation and may even have partially caused it, Obama and his AG investigate endlessly but do little. Obama is still silent.

(7) Obama "Stupidly"(To use an Obama favorite expression for those he disagrees with)---uses divisive, race-baiting Al Sharpton as his go-to consultant on race. Obama is, if anything, a master speechifier, but he is so quick to subtly and not so subtly blame, shame and try to provoke guilt especially in white Americans. As if, we all still are slave owners and abusers. I wish he would spend more time back on the south side of Chicago giving speeches about why young black persons should consider good marriages and responsible parenting. And, talk more as he did recently about imprisoned felons who have gotten it together in life.

I wish WAPO would do some real journalism about Obama.

Larry Responds

It sounds like Republicans are, as usual, too timid to even think about, let alone act, on impeachment. Obama is flouting his perceived power in a way that violates the Constitution's separation of powers.

Larry

Pete's Further Comments

Our first African American Mulatto leftwing Saul Alinsky-loving, radical president is a disgrace to his office. Not only has Obama violated his oath to defend the Constitution and our laws , but he and his minions also are seeking to undermine it! That is treason and an impeachable offense. Republican wimps are cowards in not confronting Obama and Obamaites with impeachment but are violating their oaths to "Protect and Defend" for not proposing impeachment! Even brilliant pundits like Krauthammer conflate the politically costly impeachment of Bill Clinton (Over immoral, unethical lies and dalliance with a Whitehouse intern the age of his daughter), and the failure to convict with Obama's far more serious Constitutional violating offenses. Obama's serious crimes far surpass Bill Clinton's tawdry sleaze.

Obama has consistently defamed, devalued, mocked shamed and undermined the peoples' elected representatives. His treasonous behavior feeds into the previously do-little or do-nothing image of congress, which then has progressively and now, exponentially, castrated congress even further! (A self-fulfilling prophesy thing).

Obama also betrays American representatives by going to the Anti-American and Anti-Israel United Nations to approve a treaty with our enemy (Iran) in a flagrantly cynical and toxically political way. Now he will continue as he always does (In true Alinsky style), to mock Republicans and, bully Congressional Democrats who, in cowardly fashion, pander passively to their political base of mindless liberal progressives to support their deluded, self-serving

President regardless of his arrogance.

When Obama/Kerry's logic and treaty ideas are challenged, they start using national and world-wide toxic politics to refute those who disagree, challenge and offer alternatives to their treaty agreement. Now, they say their critics are "Playing politics".

Next chapter is Obama's total hypocrisy and grandiose chastising of Kenyans who kill people for the sale of body parts of their countrymen. But here in America, Planned Parenthood operatives are collecting human "fetal" body parts to sell to research programs where government money ($75 million) goes to such medical research. (Some of the "Fetal tissue Wastes" are from Second Trimester human beings with actively developing beating hearts and tiny brains capable of experiencing terrible pain.

To top off America's Sodom and Gomorrah-like kingdom, American's interviewed on the streets don't even know the Bill of Rights or think it is passé.

Larry Thanks for hearing my ventilation and rant. I attach my essay on what politics is about psychologically. What an important time to be writing to our representatives and discussing with friends and political enemies. Some of the research has been positive, but has not been fully vetted by medical ethicists and legal authorities.

Pray for America.

Pete Olsson

Larry Wrote

Obama's rationale is simple to understand. The people in Africa are black and outside the womb. Hence, they are humans. The children in the womb are fetuses and, hence, not humans. That is why the left insists on calling these living, breathing children with souls, fetuses. That totally dehumanizes them. As a side issue, I am guessing about half of these aborted children are women. Since the left has no problem with killing thousands of living girls in the womb, who is really having the war on women?

Larry

Pete's Imagined Letter to Obama

Dear Mr. Obama

Your comment about our American Republican (And Democrat) representatives who disagree with you about your treaty agreement with Iran as being equivalent to the terrorist Mullahs in Iran is irresponsible. It is also arrogant, narcissistic and reflects paleologic, (also called predicate logic. Or lack of it!). We psychiatrists can easily spot your disordered thinking.

Your comparison is flawed and toxically 'political' and an example of predicate logic.

An example of Predicate Logic is as follows:

The predicate logic or paleologic of Obama is that the ayatollahs of Iran oppose the Obama treaty therefore U.S. Senators who oppose the Obama treaty are evil ayatollahs. Paleologic and pure demagoguery!

Peter Olsson

Larry's Response

Pete, those are great dots to connect. Whenever you give up your legitimate power to act positively, you automatically default to the other sides' rules of engagement. Giuliani cleaned up NY City. Petraeus cleaned up Iraq. Obama has given back all the territory our brave men and women shed their blood for in Iraq. What was the purpose of all those deaths and horrible wounds if we now have a president who doesn't care about America and simply hands back the hard-fought gains to the enemy? What a travesty this whole eight years are.

Larry

Pete Says

On another topic--What are your thoughts on these dots--can they be connected?

(1) In NYC Giuliani used effective assertive policing and rapport with the community by police to effectively control crime. In Iraq, after a faltering effort to control sectarian violence, General Petreous and his "Iraqi-community policing" strategy turned Iraq around before Obama snatched defeat out of the jaws of our victory. In Afghanistan and Iraq our troops constantly complain that "The Rules of Engagement" tie their hands to a dangerous degree. They must be shot at before they can fire.

(2) Obama, Holder (Ferguson) and the mayor and city attorney in Baltimore commanded police to "Stand Down" and not arrest rioters, thieves and arsonists. This policy ties their hands.

(3) Obama and DeBlasio after becoming president and NYC mayor, respectively, tend to side with Sharpton and his accusatory narrative that the police are the bad guys and they repeatedly insist that police need more and more training (i.e. blame). Obama should speak out addressing the issue of fatherless black families, unwed welfare mothers of large families of illegitimate kids and gangs that require vigorous community policing.

Are there connections of these dots as General Keane implied on Fox today?

Pete

Larry's Retort

Yes, there are connections, Pete. Obama is adept at putting up artificial straw man arguments.

He does it constantly and it is effective with the media and the people who don't pay much attention. Life rarely is about two opposite choices. There is almost always a lot of middle ground, if you seek to discover it. That makes Obama, in my view, a very shallow thinker and more of a politician than leader. He simply does not have his country's best interests at heart. He is a small minded dictatorial agitator, but then, that is his background and he has only been exposed to radicals growing up.

I would be surprised to learn that he has any positive values/beliefs reflective of traditional American values/beliefs.

Larry

Further Thoughts About Iran from Pete

Subject:**RE: Iran Redux**

Larry, I think you are right regarding Obama. Obama has set up Israel to act unilaterally and he will say our agreement with Iran forbids us to act in support of Israel. The paradox within a conundrum is that Obama's wonderful peace-seeking, faulty diplomacy makes us less safe as Obama and Kerry's unfounded cockiness will kick off a nuclear arms race (Turkey and the Saudis are already making their arrangements.)

I think Obama, in a symbolic way, is drunk with a passive sense of masochistic power analogous to his father who killed a Kenyan man while driving drunk and speeding. Then later Barack senior lost his leg while in a drunk-driving car wreck and finally died while driving drunk and rammed a large tree while speeding.(I believe it could have been a suicide). Symbolically Barack Jr. is playing passive suicide games via his use of political power over USA. Obama's father was enthralled with infidelitous sex, fast cars and drunk driving. I think that symbolically Obama is drunk-driving our country into debt and nuclear war---all the time acting like a Nobel peace prize winner. After 40+ years as a psychiatrist and psychoanalyst I have been in awe of the power of the unconscious mind that is out of balance. The more his Iran peace-making and Obamacare fails, the more intoxicated he will be with his power and the more passively suicidal Obama will become. (Just like Chamberlain---he will feel like the great man of peace)

Pete

Larry Messner Responds

To: Peter Olsson

Subject: Re: Iran Redux

Pete, the answer is simple. Pelosi set the tone with "You have to pass this bill before you can learn what is in it." Now Kerry and Obama have agreed to decrease sanctions before getting any real agreements. Where is that solid negotiator, Chamberlain, when we need him? Oh, that's right. His two sympathizers run our country.

Here is a quote from that all time, until now, great appeaser: "However much we may sympathize with a small nation confronted by big and powerful neighbors, we cannot in all circumstances undertake to involve the whole British Empire in a war simply on her account." You could easily substitute USA for British Empire and direct this quote towards Israel rather than portions of Czechoslovakia as Chamberlain intended it.

Larry

Pete Writes

Dear Larry

Obama was supposed to address America today about a deal with Iran. At this point before the prevaricator –in-chief even talks, my only question is, why do we decrease sanctions BEFORE we see those psychopaths agree to inspections. Obama says they can bring back the sanctions, "Roll back" he says if they don't comply. I will not believe a word he says.

Peter Olsson

More From Pete

I have been thinking about where America is these days in regard to politics, politicians and the close-mindedness of both sides. In fact, I wrote the following essay regarding this topic.

A Brief Classification of Closed-mindedness

As I have stated many times, "The most dangerous and vicious political battles are fought over half-truths and little lies."

Dictionary definitions appear straight-forward. But, this topic soon gets complicated.

Closed-minded: having a mind firmly unreceptive to new ideas or arguments: Is hard to argue with much less convince, a closed-minded person.

Open-minded: having or showing a mind receptive to new ideas or arguments; unprejudiced; impartial, unbigoted.]

Problems arise when topics of a lively discussion touch on challenging topics that have few absolute answers or ready access to scientific truth. These domains of discussion swirl with ambivalence and a challenge to maturity and wisdom for everyone. These topics also trigger strong emotions and readily stimulate polarized views. The more ambiguous the answer to important questions, the stronger the emotions stirred. The adage, "Never discuss religion or politics with friends or relatives" is true if one desires harmony to prevail. But, truthful discussion though often painful can allow individuals and relationships to have freedom. Loan of money and proper child rearing practices could be added to the list of problematic topics in this domain.

1---**Knee-Jerk Liberals of "The Political Left":** These folks picture themselves as elegantly open-minded, truly independent-minded, superiorly educated, exquisitely tolerant, fair to a fault, and compassionate toward the poor, uneducated, and even murderous, sadistic killers. They see crime as a result of poverty and injustice. They are always and totally against the death penalty. They advocate higher taxes especially on the rich and successful, to be used for noble causes such as foreign aid, housing and food stamps for the poor and the noble peace-keeping of the UN. They tend to read the New York Times religiously.

2---**Knee-Jerk Conservatives of "The Political Right":** These folks know they are courageously open-minded; true to freedom of the individual to succeed or fail; intolerant of condescending hand-outs to the poor; they see education as hard-earned by individuals helped by their family, and advocate firm justice toward criminal behavior. They support the death penalty and firm law and order because crime comes from bad decisions and is not primarily a psycho-social problem. They insist on sparse foreign aid with very careful accountability measures. They are highly skeptical of the United Nations and sad at its failures. They regularly read the Wall Street Journal.

3---**Independent, Undecided**, "Present", Politically Correct, or, too busy gaming and texting to notice.

Dr. Charles Krauthammer examines the Thought Police on patrol: "The left is entering a new phase of ideological agitation — no longer trying to win the debate but stopping debate altogether, banishing from public discourse all opposition. The proper word for that attitude is totalitarian. It declares certain controversies over and visits serious consequences — from social ostracism to vocational defenestration — upon those who refuse to be silenced... To oppose it is nothing but bigotry, akin to racism."

Larry Replies

Brilliant summation Pete. You, unfortunately, have interpreted all the moves by all the players precisely correct. Santayana was right as we have all said. Those who forget the past are condemned to repeat it. I don't think, however, that anyone has forgotten the past and are now running blithely ahead in ignorance. Iran certainly isn't. I am sure Russia will never forget Hitler and China is too close geographically to Japan to forget that country's military advances in WWII. That leaves the West. Here I see us as willing dupes. While many of us haven't forgotten WWII, too many, led by Obama, are acting like we have. I see Obama as the person leading this ill-fated parade. He is all about himself and a legacy that he believes is tied into an Iran deal. Any deal.

I am visiting friends at this time. I had polite conversations with two of them. One blamed the homeless problem on Reagan, although the homeless became that way from the 1960's on because of liberal policies that said they had rights NOT to be in mental health institutions. When discussing Obamacare and I said it had been passed behind closed doors, no Republicans had participated, and Pelosi said you must pass this bill to find out what is in it, another liberal said all of that is a lie. None of it happened. What is my point? This is how liberals act. They simply deny the actual truth to spin what they want everyone to now believe.

Hence, I see Obama playing the same pied piper song. Ignore the past. I will tell you what it is, and it isn't what happened. Deny the past. Then believe my version and follow me into the future. This is all deliberate and is being portrayed and presented by a president who cares only about himself. It is not just a sad time for America and the Western World, it is a dangerous time. If a solid, strong conservative isn't elected president and the Senate doesn't stay Republican, we could very well see the end of America in many ways. We are at a crossroads and too many people don't see it or don't care. Too many don't even know what is happening or refuse to get involved.

Pete, you were so right when you say today's youth are only interested in their Starbucks, i-phones, etc. The ultimate liberal car, the Prius, is virtually everywhere out here. I see them at every turn. I would guess they make up over 10% of all cars on the road in CA. This is how liberals think. If they have their toys, they believe the world is super okay. They will drive off the cliff in their Prius while sipping a latte mocha supremo and texting on their i-phone.

Larry

Pete Writes

Yesterday I heard and saw Britain's foreign minister announce the re-opening of the UK

Embassy in Tehran, Iran after he talked with Iran's counterpart. I was immediately reminded of Nevil Chamberlin's "Peace in Our Time" fiasco after his talk and "Deal" with Hitler. The Brit expressed the "Hope" that such progress as the nuclear deal will welcome Iran into the world of civilized nations.

The above announcement is made before our congress approves of the 'treaty' or rejects it. I think this is Obama's international playing of politics to try to get his bogus treaty through. The Brits who want trade with Iran and its oil, collaborates with Obama's give-away, bad deal with Iran.

In addition, Iran this weekend boasted of already planned deals with Russia to get long range ballistic missiles and anti-aircraft rockets from Russia to shoot down American and Israeli war planes that would bomb Iran's nuclear weapons sites if (Really WHEN) Iran violates the deal and with the billions they get in the deal Iran will proceed with funding of Hezbollah, and other terror projects.

If unlikely bed-fellows like Mussolini, Togo and Hitler could cooperate to try for world dominance in WWII, what or who is keeping Iran, N Korea, Russia, Homegrown terrorist nests and even China from joining pragmatic forces toward power and control while Europe, America and the rest of the "Free World" sleeps?

Economic dominance of the 21st century AXIS Powers will blend with pseudo olive branches of phony peace postures.

I think WWIII is a stealth, asymmetrical war of small cuts, scratches and economic defeats of The West.

I hope I am wrong and the KOOM-BY-YAH love songs of international harmony of UK, France, Germany, Obama/ Kerry are successful.

I sense sadly that Iran and 21st century AXIS power colleagues don't share Obama and UK's vision of History's new turn toward peace and a nuclear deal as currently envisioned.

Pete Olsson

Pete Comments on Pretentious Nobility

Nothing "Noble" or regal about hateful, arrogant, haughty, destructive and crude-mouthed King Noble a Black Supremecist. I have been watching his U-Tube videos and I believe his hate speech is a symbolically connected to Eric Holder, Al Sharpton, and Barack Obama's subtle, persistent, biased, word-worshipping speeches, actions and lack of actions. Obama starts with candy-coated or shaming-blaming admonishments for peace and goodwill, but then talks about "All the work America must do to further expunge our phantom persistent RACISM." Obama's plausible denial of his unconscious and conscious messages of race-baiting is increasingly impossible. Obama needs to be on the South side of Chicago and West side near Woods street----Not Alaska touting his shaming, blaming shibboleths about climate change.

Obama would have Americans to have fewer guns, just when devils like King Noble makes it important for us to have them to protect ourselves. We each need a gun and know how to use it safely! And carefully learn what areas to avoid if we live near or in big cities. Black lives matter much less when black people spew hate speech like King Noble or KKKers.

What is so frustrating, exasperating and at times enraging to me about Obama is the way he doesn't come right out about his negativity toward Christianity. Obama uses scripture and allusions to scripture for his own political purposes, (I see that as "Taking God's name in vain"---a Judeo-Christian commandment) and leaves his herds of secular, progressive, lawyer minions to execute his anti-Christian shaming, blaming and subtle persecutions on America. Obama even joins the pope in a subtle politically correct condemnation of "Evil Capitalism". The vast heard of Obamaists in America don't even seem to grasp the subliminal but powerful Anti-American messaging.

Pete Olsson

Larry's Response to Pete

Totally correct, Pete. Obama is truly a wolf in sheep's clothing. He hides and prevaricates and lies about his true self and his beliefs. The sad thing for America is how many people are taken in by him and, now, Hillary. While her numbers are dropping, I see today where she would beat Trump head to head. Trump may be bombastic, but he is a patriot and hasn't killed anyone (Benghazi) or acted treasonously (selling 20% of our uranium to Russia) like the god-awful Hillary.

Larry

Pete Speaks Further

Larry

What fascinates me to think about is---What is "Education" when it comes to politics?

I thought further and conclude that in our "Modern *CULTURE OF NARCISSISM* and

Me, ME Me- ness, the adage of Lyndon Johnson applies. i.e. "The president needs to figure out where the people are headed, then run out in front in that direction and yell, "FOLLOW ME"! I think both Obama and Trump have figured out and or intuited the most effective applications of Johnson's conman law and Alinsky's tactics to contemporary politics. The implication seems to be that in America lately, the dope smoking, Hollywood-adoring, narcissistic majority or the angry formerly silent majority has to be fired-up with self-placating, self-soothing, feel good platitudes and slogans. Obama has successfully hood-winked, hornswoggled and manipulated Americans in a way that placates their fear of war, appeals to a Shallow sense of compassion or pseudo-compassion for "Poor" immigrants down trodden blacks, and he has done this very successfully at taxpayer's expense! Trump seems to have turned the former "Silent Majority" (ala Nixon, Agnew) into a new enthused aggressive vocal majority in love with his bold, self-confident, bombastic style. No steadier good guy Bushes, Romneys, solid old-fashioned good, truly god-fearing and respecting honorable guys like McCain, Scott Walker, Bobby Jindal, Mitt Romney, Mike Huckaby, Bush, are perceived as passé, square, not 'with it', un-cool and out-of-touch.

Hopefully a Fiorina, Carson, Christie or Kasich can break the Trumpian and Obamaist spells.

Paradoxically, the brash, narcissistic, illegal power moves and manipulations of

Obama have some people thinking that AT LEAST GOT THINGS DONE. Trump is trying to beat Obama at his own narcissistic game but with a uber P.T. Barnum modern style.

Scary.

Pete Olsson

Barack Obama's View of History and America in the World: Liminal and Subliminal Messages by Peter Olsson

Obama said, "They get bitter, they cling to guns or religion or antipathy to people who aren't like them or anti-immigrant sentiment or anti-trade sentiment as a way to explain their frustrations."

So said Barack Obama about jobless workers in old mid- west industrial towns during his campaign on April, 14, 2008.

The Context of Obama's World View

Barack Obama's comments about History, The World and America's role are intriguing because they, like Obama, are a cognitive and political palimpsest*. The author thinks that Obama will never be candid about what he really thinks about the essence of the world and America. Let's speculate. In listening to and observing Obama, the listener must both pay careful attention to the Teleprompter lines and, as best as possible, between Obama's lines. Over time Obama has both radically changed between his lines (subtext), and, not changed at all in his lines of communication about History and America.

Conservative critics of Obama approach his administration as if it constantly falls short of the general way American presidents generally perform or are expected to think, behave, and act. The author believes that Obama, as his wife Michelle has said, "He's a dreamer". (See *Dreams From My Father.*)

Obama and The Power of His Words

Obama believes in the profound power of his thoughts and particularly his words.

David Maraniss, in his book about Obama, describes Barack's comment as the English class of Ms. Czurles-Nelson at Punahou School in Hawaii discussed what people fear the most.

Obama said,

"WORDS...words are the power to be feared most...whether directed personally or internationally, words can be weapons of destruction."

As one observes Obama's verbal skills in action, it is impressive how he entwines graceful movements, a winsome smile, and a smooth charm that accompanies his powerful staccato -wielding of words. His verbal-based charisma is significantly connected to the timing of his rising and falling baritone voice. These seem studied and resemble other influential speakers like Bill Clinton, Martin Luther King, John Kennedy, and Billy Graham. Barack Obama Jr. seems spellbound by the omnipotent fantasy of the imagined pure power of his words. "As If" the programs he would establish and their successful results were already on record. How could anyone disagree with the smooth magic of Obama's words?

*Palimpsest; a very old document or painting on which the original writing or painting has been erased and replaced with new writing or a canvas painted over with a new scene. The meaning of the writing or painting has changed over time.

Obama's Concept of History

Obama talks about History in an idealized, romantic, wistful, yet simultaneously didactic way. Obama seems to think he somehow knows best the way History should inevitably unfold with the greatest good for the greatest number of people. Obama chides Putin and Assad, for example, for acting out of line with the right, good, rational or best course of History. Obama's view of the inevitable and best course of History seems to come from a beneficent, idealized, and utopian peoples-paradise location. Obama alludes to a hopefully perfectible future. His favorite wistful expression about domestic or foreign issues is, "We have a lot of work to do". The paradise of History Obama alludes to is without racism, discrimination, materialism, pollution, greed, war, or natural disaster. Science and democratic government can even in time, make the Earth's environment safe, even perfect. Obama speaks of evil but seems to underestimate its stubborn power and inevitability.

In the History Obama insists on, "everyone gets a fair shot". Niccolo Machiovelli, Mao, Stalin, Pol Pot, Hitler, Assad, Putin, and other bullies are simply not allowed in Obama's playground of History. In due time , Obama will lead in a benevolent march toward a world exactly like the 1949 International Declaration of Human Rights of the United Nation's as envisioned by Eleanor Roosevelt.

Barack Obama's Underlying View of America

Obama seems, on the surface of his word-canvas for America's portrait, to hold us to a high standard. Yet, there is a deeper, subliminal tone of dark disappointment in America. America is not really exceptional. We are shameful, greedy, selfish and needing to be brought down more than a peg from our high horses.

Americans cruelly held and abused slaves and still need to seek reconciliation. We still don't treat black persons with fairness, dignity and respect. Shame on America! Shame on our police! Our collective guilt stems from collective racism, bigotry and unfairness. Such dark fires of hate still to simmer in the American soul. We abused, bullied and mistreated Native Americans. They deserve perpetual recompense. All good Americans must compassionately share our wealth with other Americans who can't work and who feel like they don't get a fair chance. And America, about those poor Mexicans, Central Americans and South Americans, welcome those poor, struggling folks to find prosperity in our wonderful land of opportunity and brotherhood. We don't need walls, fences and border guards, we out of collective guilt should welcome them to compensate for all our colonialism and exploitation of their countries. And Africans, Syrians, Libyans, we have broad shoulders and deep pockets. We are even willing to go even further in debt to help you poor folks as well.

And Those Christians!

America, you should be ashamed, especially you cruel Christians who oppose gay marriage, abortion, or find problems with paying for corrective surgery for transsexuals. American Christians should give more respect and deference to atheists, so they can have free expression and hone their skills talents and legal prerogatives. Christians, your shame should drive you in droves to church to pray for forgiveness. Particularly for The Inquisition and those horrible, vicious crusades!

And Those Guns of Mass Killers

Mr. Obama reacted about the Oregon mass killing before any information was available about the killer, his guns, or other details such as the fact that there was only one unarmed security person on the school campus. Obama tried to politicize the event and seems to take each mass killing as a personal issue. For Obama all things personal seem to easily get conflated with political. He even lied about his mother's health insurance to promote his Obamacare program. Such impulsive verbal behavior is a repeated pattern for Obama who thinks his words and gun law policy recommendations would magically solve the mass murder and gun violence issue. Obama never speaks about the black on black gun- use carnage on the south side of Chicago where he was a community organizer. Hardly a single murder in Chicago would be prevented by stricter gun laws alone. Obama's essential silence about police officer killings says volumes.

The Military

Though Obama praises and complements our military at every photo op, he has let our military strength decline and alludes to the foolish use of our military power. Especially bad are Americans George Bush and Dick Cheney. Obama seems to imply that America has been a bully. Our military power should not be used for strength that legitimizes diplomacy and creates peace. America must perpetually turn-the-other-cheek and proceed constantly with "diplomacy", rationality, cooperation with "partners". Obama's America only uses military force as the last resort, which for Obama never seems to occur despite red lines he draws.

Americans, we held our awesome and terrible nuclear power over the heads of the poor Japanese, Chinese, North Koreans, Iranians, Russians and the rest of the world long enough. Now we need to spread good will and extend ourselves as a role model of peace, love and understanding. So, when Iran and other nations get their nuclear arms to equal our stocks, then, we can all be good boys and girls and rationally agree to a nuclear arms free world.

Conclusion:

Watching President Obama confer with Putin at the UN it is amazing to read Obama's non-verbal and verbal behavior. Obama exudes a weird mixture of obsequiousness and arrogance. But in street terms, Obama is chicken.

So, America, don't be bewildered or troubled by Obama and Kerry's smiles and nuanced dances with words of peace and compromise with Iran and Putin at the UN. Obama is not failing as American president. These events are proceeding exactly along the trail of "Hope and Change" as Obama promised. And be comforted, Pope Francis supports Obama and prays for us.

Larry's Response

Brilliantly spot on. Pete. One of my favorite comments of yours.

Larry

Larry Speaks on Krauthammer

Hi Pete,

Charles Krauthammer is right on point. When Obama became president in 2008, recall the map and political leaders in the Mideast. The war in Iraq had been won. We had 157,800 troops in Iraq in early 2009 at the start of Obama's presidency. As we all know, Obama withdrew all troops from Iraq in spite of his military advisers telling him that he needed to keep a minimum of 20-30,000 to maintain our victory. He ignored their advice and subsequently snatched defeat from the jaws of victory. As a leader he is a dunderhead and as a military strategist he is completely over his head and clueless.

Libya's leader Muammar Al-Quaddafi, Egypt's leader Hosni Mubarak, Syria's leader Bashar Al-Assad were all evil men, but they had a calming effect on their country, albeit from an iron fisted manner. There was no ISIS. In spite of everything, the Mideast was a lot calmer and safer than it is today. Israel was still our strongest ally and, under Bush and all previous presidents, we remained its staunchest defender.

Fast forward to today. Iraq has been totally lost. All the blood, weapons, money and lives lost there were pointless as Obama gave up all our hard fought and won victories and gave the country to the terrorists. Libya is lost as Obama stood by and let its leader be assassinated and the country turn into total chaos beginning with allowing our ambassador Stephens and three seals to be tortured and butchered as he stood by, went to bed, and traveled to Las Vegas for a selfish campaign event. Hillary did likewise.

Egypt had its Spring event and Obama stood by and fiddled. For a long time it was lost to the terrorists. And, of course, Syria exploded and, while Obama drew invisible red lines he once again ignored the use of WMD by Assad and sat on his hands. The result of all this? ISIS was founded and is now flourishing. But the biggest loss is our total influence in a region where we once held sway as the strongest outside force. Obama capitulated to Putin who now is the undisputed outside leader and influence in the Mideast for the first time in decades. All this has happened under Obama's nose and with his tacit approval.

Larry

Pete Answwers

Thank you, Larry,

The facts that you and Krauthammer summarize define the dreamer utopian Folly of

Obama's foreign policy. And future chapters beyond Obama's muddling's will embolden ISIS and Iran's allies like Hezbollah to attack Israel and our country.

The other day I heard a commentator say that the European officials have found no ISIS or Al Qaeda agents among the thousands and thousands of Syrian migrants.

I guess none were wearing ISIS tee shirts as they streamed across the borders.

Pete

Pete's Letter to President Obama

Dear Mr. President

Thank you for your detailed reply to my concerns. Sadly, I guess we will have to agree to disagree. (Have you read Senator Chuck Schumer's thoughts about the Iran deal?)

In my opinion you are wrong about the assessment of opportunities for a new basis for a positive relationship between the free world and Iran. You seem to have psychological blind spots about the ominous new Axis of Evil developing between Iran. Russia, Iraq and Assad's Syria/Hezbollah.

You also seem to conflate any increase of firm demands about Iran's terror talk and actions, increased sanctions on Iran, and positioning of our military presence in Europe with some kind of all-out war. I think Iran, Russia and Assad only respect military-based diplomatic power---not lectures, shaming and scolding about what is the best nature of History's best and benevolent unfolding. I sense that it is not Putin's weakness but your own weakness and psychological blind spots that are involved. You boast about your commanding the most powerful military in the world but you seem timid about greatly bolstering it and leading it to a position of strength that is more likely to gain greater peace in the world.

Sincerely yours

Peter A. Olsson MD

The White House Response

Thank you for writing. After two years of negotiations, the United

States—together with our international partners—has achieved what decades of animosity has not: a comprehensive, long-term deal that will verifiably prevent Iran from obtaining a nuclear weapon. This deal shows that American leadership and diplomacy can bring real and meaningful change that makes our country and our world safer and more secure. We negotiated from a position of strength and principle, and the result is a nuclear deal that cuts off every pathway to a nuclear weapon. I want to make sure you know what this deal means and how it works.

Under this deal, Iran will not be able to produce highly enriched uranium or weapons-grade plutonium—the raw materials necessary to build a bomb. Iran will reduce its stockpile of enriched uranium by 98 percent and remove two-thirds of its installed centrifuges—the machines necessary to produce highly enriched uranium—and store them under constant international supervision. To put that in perspective, Iran currently has a uranium stockpile that could produce up to 10 nuclear weapons, and that stockpile will be reduced to a fraction of what would be required for a single weapon. Additionally, Iran will modify its nuclear reactor in Arak so it cannot produce weapons-grade plutonium, and all spent fuel from the reactor will be shipped out of the country indefinitely.

This deal is not built on trust; it's built on verification. For the first time, we will be in a position to verify that Iran is meeting all of these commitments. International nuclear inspectors will have access to Iran's nuclear program where and when necessary. This is the most comprehensive and intrusive verification regime we have ever negotiated. If Iran tries to divert raw materials to covert facilities, inspectors will be able to access any suspicious locations. As Iran implements this deal, it will receive gradual relief from sanctions, and if it violates any aspect of this agreement, sanctions that have crippled Iran's economy will snap back into place.

That's the deal. It has the full backing of the international community. Without it, there would be no agreed-upon limitations on Iran's nuclear program, and other countries would feel more compelled to pursue their own programs—threatening a nuclear arms race in the most volatile region of the world. Put simply, no deal means a greater chance of more war in the Middle East. That is why it would be irresponsible to walk away from this deal.

Moving forward, I welcome a robust debate in Congress on the details of this agreement. As Commander-in-Chief, I am confident that this deal will meet the national security interests of the United

States and our allies, so I will veto any legislation that prevents its successful implementation.

Our differences with Iran are real, and the difficult history between our nations cannot be ignored—but it is possible to change. The path of violence and rigid ideology—a foreign policy based on threats to attack neighbors or eradicate Israel—is a dead end. A different path of tolerance and peaceful resolution of conflict leads to more integration into the global economy, more engagement with the international community, and the ability of the Iranian people to prosper and thrive. This deal offers an opportunity to move in a new direction, and we should seize it.

Again, thank you for writing. To learn more about this historic deal and how it will make the United States, our allies, and our world safer, please visit www.WhiteHouse.gov/Iran-Deal.

Sincerely,

Barack Obama

Pete's Follow-Up with Larry

Speaking psychological truth to power can be positive depending on the wisdom of the person in power. PAO

Larry

In my opinion, Obama more than most politicians speaks words loaded with obfuscation, prevarication, and very crafty shaming, blaming, scolding and he is surprisingly rigid and judgmental in his eloquently crafted speeches. I wish I or another good psychoanalyst could have spent several hundred hours with him in the late 1990s and then again when his book *DREAMS FROM MY FATHER,* when it first came out.

Of course, as Eugene McCarthy once said to me---everyone running for president should have quality time spent with a psychoanalyst; but, then they would probably not become a candidate. I'll never forget his smile as he said that.

By-the-way Eugene McCarthy's book of poems is outstanding.

Pete

A Critic Responds to Pete

DEAR CRITIC of my criticism of Obama's IRAN DEAL

If you choose to read the monograph I sent, you will find that the five years I spent researching the unconscious, emotional factors behind and beneath presidential decision-making was not anti-pragmatic but rather a different domain of perspective on decision-making. There is a whole section on the purely rational, traditional pragmatic "Realpolitik" as Kissinger called it. The two domains are not mutually exclusive. I would argue that politicians on both sides of things are often blinded by their own unconscious blind spots that are human and ubiquitous. It merely helps to be as free from the constrictions of unconscious conflict and insecurity while making pragmatic decisions that affect the survival of the world. For example---One of us consulted daily with Carter during Camp David peace talks. One of our consultants had helped Kennedy with the potentially crippling "Group Think" that almost blew up the Cuban Missile Crisis. Our five year think tank experience was the second most important experience of my career. The first was working with our POWs returning from the Hanoi Hilton. That was when I met John McCain and some of his brave colleagues.

I certainly agree that I may have a more romantic and idealistic view of how I might contribute to helping Obama with clearing the field of Obama's decision-making. But, in the roaring winds of political conflict lately, I thought it was worth a try.

Many years ago, I had a fascinating experience with Eugene McCarthy. Several of us spent two hours with him discussing the Vietnam War decisions. He was a fascinating, fun and brilliant political philosopher. He joked with us saying that any person who wants to be president is troubled psychologically and needs to spend time in productive conversation with a good psychoanalyst. Then he said---"If the conversation was deep enough the candidate might change his or her mind about running". He also felt that a triumvirate of people should run for president. Two women and one man. We asked why---he said the foreign, domestic and military arenas were too difficult for one person. He said, "There would also be fewer wars and when war was necessary we would get out sooner. He also felt the budget would be more reasonable".

It was an interesting discussion.

Pete

The critic then said Obama would not accept a consultation with Pete, who replied, in turn, below:

DEAR CRITIC: Somewhat "Tongue-in-Cheek"

If Obama looked up my credentials and his staff interviewed me they would value the project. I sent you previously the full published article I sent him about his specific issues if you care to read it. See (pp 67-81 of this book)

Peter

The Critic Responded

No elected official will agree to a therapy session from a complete stranger, regardless of credentials, and that's what you appear to want to do. Informing Obama of his psychological blind spots is not talking about issues.

I think the critic is reflecting the painful political divisions in American society. The national debate has grown more than coarse. Example Trumps comments about fellow candidates and the liberal media's recent obscene and crude insults towards Ben Carson. As my fear and anxiety about America builds---I think the divisions are not totally caused by, but are definitely fueled by Obama who way too frequently impulsively speaks out about highly charged issues. Obama initially says we need more information, discussion and investigations but then pronounces his judgment before a study or investigation is even complete.

I fear our country is teetering on the edge of losing all basis in rational civil discussion.

Thus the 2016 election has become the natural turning point of our American large group's history. I perceive echoes like at the time of the civil war which escalated into scape-goating of friends, neighbors and families with horrible results.

Pete Olsson

Pete's Observations of an Obama TV interview

Larry

I carefully watched Steve Croft's interview of Barack Obama this evening. Here are my observations:

1) Steve Croft did an excellent job particularly about foreign policy. Croft stood tall, didn't flinch, interrupted when he needed to and asked clear, pointed and excellent questions.

2) In discussing foreign policy Obama looked and sounded pitiful and out-of-touch to the point of being overtly in denial. I think he is in a bubble of unreality. In domestic political areas of questioning, Obama seemed clever, sly and smoothly "Political" and astute.

3) Medically, Obama seems to have lost more weight and grown grayer. I think he is depressed in the fashion that narcissistic persons do. He showed a haughty, sarcastic, aloof and arrogant, cocky style so typical of narcissistic persons in their protective bubble.

4) When Croft pointedly challenged Obama about how dangerous Putin's increasing dominance seemed to diminish America and Obama's leadership. Obama split-off into a comment

about how the real danger in the world is climate change! Obama seemed detached, dreamy and possibly pandering to the ultra-left.

5) I am amazed by Obama's relentless insecurity and self-protective haughtiness as he asked Croft, "Is that all you got, Steve?" and done with a smarmy smile as if the questions were beneath him and unprofessional.

God help us if this man doesn't get jolted back to reality

Peter Olsson

Larry Responds

You're so right Pete. Words pale without definitive actions. Words can inspire (witness FDR and Churchill during WWII. JFK in his inaugural. Reagan almost daily. Sadly, Hitler) but they only inspire because they precipitated and preordained action. Without military, economic and moral strength to back up grandiose words, they fall flat and soon become just background noise.

Unfortunately, Obama's words have become the din and static drowning out real active voices. (If you like your doctor you can keep your doctor. His "red line" speech for Assad. etc. etc.). He remains an empty suit and barrel rattling around in his own self-assured grandiosity. History will treat him with disdain in time.

Larry

Pete on Obama's Wordiness

WORDS, WORDS, WORDS

Obama again suffers from the fantasy that his grandiose words define the flow of History. He believes his words are equal to our strategy in Afghanistan and prevent the course of Putin's march across boundaries. Obama acts as if his job is entirely to give speeches about our diplomatic agendas, our military strategies and tactics. He never discusses the war in Syria or Afghanistan---what exactly is our plan? How is it going? And, most importantly, how will America stay safe if we don't actively lead with boots on the ground to destroy ISIS, Al Qaeda and their Islamist terrorists in the Taliban.

Obama's major creative effort seems to plan details of the underlying political domain behind decisions rather than time spent governing, administrating and leading. WORDS don't equal leadership. Action does. And, action is not solely all-out war.

Pete

Larry Discusses Obama's Deficient Leadership

At this point in time, I believe we need a strong, Conservative leader.

I heard a partial interview with Craig Hulet yesterday. Craig B Hulet was both speech writer and Special Assistant for Special Projects to Congressman Jack Metcalf (Retired). He has been a consultant to federal law enforcement ATF&E of Justice/Homeland Security for over 20 years. Hulet served in Vietnam 1969-70, 101st Airborne, C Troop 2/17th Air Cav and graduated third in his class at Aberdeen Proving Grounds Ordnance School MOS 45J20 Weapons. He remains a paid analyst and consultant in various areas of geopolitical, business and security issues.

What he said was scary and all too possible. To paraphrase him, he said America is at a point in time and circumstance that we are extremely weak in so many ways. For example, militarily Russia has a standing army of 3-5 million. China has around a 10-million-man army. We have less than 500,000 and many of our army troops have been on multiple deployments to Iraq and Afghanistan. Some as many as nine deployments. They are worn out.

To use a football analogy, if the offense is weak the defense will be called upon over and over again until it is worn down. Obama has weakened our military's offensive capabilities and now our defense is too weak. I recall when I was in the Air Force that the concept was to have a superior conventional military capability to prevent a nuclear war. If we could beat any enemy in a conventional war, there was no need to use nukes. Well, Obama has destroyed our conventional capability. We are at the lowest level of our military since pre-WWII.

If we get engaged in a conventional war (What would happen if either Russia or we shoot down the other's warplane or bomb their troops while fighting in Syria?) with Russia, we could not win. Period! God forbid that China opens a second front in the South China Sea by sinking one of our warships who they think is violating their newly declared oceanic territorial rights around their newly built islands. We could not beat Russia or China alone and if they combine in two wars we are burnt toast. Our only option is to go nuclear. That is why we have to elect a solid Conservative as our next president and rebuild our military.

Peace is not maintained through weakness. It is preserved through superior military might so no one dares to attack. Of course, we are in a new method of war with the Islamic Terrorists which means we need to have multiple tactics and concepts to maintain peace, but unilaterally disarming in the face of Russia and Chinese aggression and Islamic Terrorists is insane and can only lead to our demise.

Sadly, the clock is ticking and while our enemies grow stronger, we grow weaker under this failed leader. As the title of a book I read long ago states (Khrushchev era)," The Future is Ours Comrade "by Joseph Novak and it is much truer now than then.

Larry

Larry Writes to Obama

Dear President Obama,

In light of the massive, destructive and murderous terror attack on Paris, France last night by Radical Islamic Terrorists, I urge you to finally name our enemy in the most clear, definitive manner. This is not work place violence as you misnamed the Fort Hood attack. Call it what it is. Support French President Hollande when he declared this an act of war and that his response would be merciless. Show the same fortitude he is displaying.

You need to end your naïve and dangerous policy and tactic of retreat in the face of this worldwide caliphate. ISIS is NOT the Jayvee as you wrongly and illogically called them. Even as recently as the morning before the devastating attack on the freedom loving people of Paris and France, you incorrectly said that ISIS was contained and not a real global threat. Are you still prepared to stand by that mistaken statement?

Leading from behind, as you constantly and dangerously do, is not the answer. You have been proven wrong again and again by failing to listen to your military experts. Further, while it is evident from your dastardly deed of returning the bust of Sir Winston Churchill to the English Ambassador as one of your first acts as President, you would be wise to heed this true leader's advice when he said, in the midst of World War II, "We shall defend our island, whatever the cost may be, we shall fight on the beaches, we shall fight on the landing grounds, we shall fight in the fields and in the streets, we shall fight in the hills; we shall never surrender." Are you now willing to do the same?

Additionally, I call upon you to reverse your reckless decision to allow countless thousands of Syrian refugees into this country. One of last night's terrorists was carrying a Syrian passport. Your misguided idea of humanitarianism must not trump the need for America's safety and security.

If you cannot or will not stand up for America now in this time of her need, please resign and let a leader who possesses the courage, foresight and willingness you apparently lack to step forward in your place.

Regards,

Laurence F. Messner, Lt Col USAF (Retired)

Hampton, NH

Pete Replies

Great letter! It speaks for many, many Americans.

Pete

Pete to Larry on the Cult of Osama

In my 2007 book--THE CULT OF OSAMA; Psychoanalyzing Osama bin Laden and his Magnetism For Muslim Youths---pp51-53 I summarized the 40-year plan of Al Qaeda and the Muslim Brotherhood. Hassan Turabi who got his law degree at U of Paris held a conference in Khartoum Sudan. In attendance was Bin Laden, Zawahiri and other radical Sunni Muslim terrorists. Their game plan is right on schedule!! ISIS rather than the JV is really the modernized, social mediatized form of Islamofascist Muslim youth. Our "Modern American youth faces the challenge moving beyond Obamaism's politically correct utopianism and denial of the war ISIS has declared against us. Obama's cowardly, politically safe drone strikes only stirs the ISIS hornets' nest. Each Osama killed by an Obama drone strike will quickly be replaced by another youthful fanatic.

After they cripple Europe,Israel and America are close behind in their master-plan.

Our JV president would not even go to Paris to march in unity with other world leaders after the Charlie H murders. Obama would not even send his VP or Sec of State to march. Obama's veneer of Christianity and unconscious soul of Islam will destroy America if he doesn't refuse Syrian immigrants and start securing our border as France has just done and maybe it's already too late.

I agree Larry. We all need to write to our reps. America needs to wake up starting with leadership in the Whitehouse and our failing universities where the real climate threat is the attitudes and pc of many students whose pot smoking and immaturity will destroy their /our future.

Pete Olsson

Pete Writes to President Obama

Dear Mr. Obama

I do not understand your constant denial about America and the civilized world in an all-out war against radical Muslim Islamo-Fascism. Osama bin Laden, Zawahiri and Turabi planned their war against Jews and Christians in Khartoum, Sudan in 1993. Their plan is right on schedule. ISIL has declared war on America and today, they say America is next.

This is a spiritual, ideological, military and religious war, not merely a law enforcement issue! Your stubborn position about this issue is wrong. We have not contained much less destroyed ISIL.

I believe that you must halt any plans to welcome migrants from Syria to America immediately. Despite your spokesman's assurance that Syrian immigrants can be thoroughly vetted is nonsense. As a physician psychiatrist and psychoanalyst who has interviewed many prospective violent or suicidal persons I can tell you it takes an educated guess. Even if US officials took an extensive psycho-social, vocational, spiritual and religious history, the successful vetting of thousands and thousands of immigrants is impossible.

American leadership means confronting so called peaceful and moderate Muslims around America and the world to reform their religion. For peaceful Muslims to stay passive about the needed reformation of their religion and calling out their violent brothers and sisters is tacit approval of Islamo-Fascist terrorism.

Peter A. Olsson MD

Larry Discusses Obama

I have been struggling for years trying to decide whether Obama is intelligent and competent, but simply wrong, or whether he is incompetent. After his press conference, I can honestly say I am beginning to come down on the side of incompetence and his bluster and constant verbal attacks on Republicans are his method of attempting to cover up that incompetency. He truly does not know he does not know. I teach that that is the most difficult leadership stage to grow out of because you don't know you are in it and you may actually believe you are smarter than you actually are. It normally takes an outside force to draw you outward and upward. Rarely can it be done by the individual alone. It usually takes an outside significant event to occur for an individual to grow out of this stage and up to the next one of Conscious Incompetence, whereby you know you don't know. And that is so true of Obama.Yet, when a significant event in the world occurs, as it did Fri in Paris, Obama simply cannot use it to learn and grow. He is Peter Principled out. He has risen to his own personal level of incompetence. Unfortunately for America and the world at large, his incompetence is a danger to all of us.

Larry

Pete Responds to Larry

Your further thoughts about Obama's smarts and competence is brilliant! I conclude the same from my psychoanalytic perspective.

The most dangerous physicians and nurses I have known during my career were those who "Didn't know what they didn't know."

Obama's pathological narcissism leads to his arrogant unawareness of what he doesn't know and his lack of the empathy and curiosity about himself that it would take for him to know what he doesn't know.

He is not a complete cunning psychopath or flagrantly psychotic but unaware of his unawareness. That is why he comes across as too cool for school until he is appropriately confronted with the reality of what he doesn't know. A regal chameleon can't see what color he really is because his throne and robes are always gold in his mind's eye.

Pete

Pete Comments Further

Larry

The public statements by Obama and Kerry regarding the ISIS attacks in Paris are stunning. Surrealistic. For Obama to perfunctorily express sadness and empathy for the French and then talk about the armed assault in Paris as a mere "Set-back" along the road of his brilliant plan to contain and then destroy ISIS is pitiful. (I recall with anger when Obama did not go to Paris after the Charlie Hebdo killings or even send his VP!) Obama's outrageous, sarcastic, arrogant, shaming, blaming attacks on Republicans as alleged enemies of America is also pitiful. It is Obama's stupid verbal attacks on Americans who disagree with him that aid ISIS and global Muslim Islamofascism which threatens Christianity, Jews and peaceful Muslims.

Then Kerry fumbles around verbally but basically saying the Charlie Hebdo attacks were "Understandable", "A rationale"/ "Legitimacy" as opposed to the recent act of war against Paris by ISIS. There is a flimsy logic to his comparison but a deeper implication is that Paris and The West bears some responsibility for causing brutal ISIS attacks. Radical IslamoFascists of all vintages have declared war on us! I think Kerry smoked to much Pot in his youth. It damaged his cognitive processes and judgment. I have experienced an on-going debate in my mind for seven years along these lines Is Obama naive? Stupid? Incompetent? In massive denial about reality and his role as POTUS? Frankly delusional? Calculatedly changing America into a Obamaist utopia?

Larry, I conclude that Obama's Narcissistic character leads to what you astutely call Obama's inability to know what he doesn't know. Obama can't bear to become aware of his lack of awareness or mindfulness of his failure to be a leader. When the stress of valid criticism accumulates toward Obama he suffers subtle fragmentation of his self. That leads to his narcissistic defenses of grandiosity, arrogance, haughtiness and denial about how he projects his inner narcissistic rage on to his critics.

I think Muslim IslamoFascists all over the world sense their opportunity to exploit the leader of the free world's weakness and vulnerability. The war against us will only grow worse over the next year. Fear will affect our economy, travel to Europe and safety in US cities. Even if Russia, Germany, France fill the gap in The West's fight against Radical Islam, our country's success and safety will be affected.

Pete

Larry's Comeback

Absolutely correct Pete. Instead of using a high level of Emotional Intelligence (EI) and debating the issues based on facts and ideas (Let the best solution win the day) he reverts to a very low level of EI and verbally attacks and belittles his opponents who have the audacity to question him.

Let me share a quote from one of the texts I use on EI. It comes from the book, *Leadership in Healthcare* by Carson Dye. "Emotional

Intelligence is the subset of social intelligence that involves the ability to monitor one's own and others' feelings and emotions, to discriminate among them and to use this information to guide one's thinking and actions. Emotional intelligence has two components: energy and maturity. .Maturity refers to people's refinement, social graces, tact, **capacity to grow and change** and ability to interpret signals from others. It reminds leaders to **apologize, express gratitude, harbor no ill will,** empathize, have a sense of humor and **respect others.** Also, maturity keeps leaders poised during times of distress and wise during times of pressure." The emphasis is mine.

Compare that definition and description with the actions of Obama. He is the polar opposite of a highly Emotional Intelligent leader. I believe I will write to him and explain, in a professional way, that he needs to develop a higher level of EI, as both America and the world need this from the world's purported most powerful leader. I seriously doubt that he will understand the concept of EI, as he does not practice it in the least, but perhaps someone on his staff will read my letter and do some research into EI and help our not very illustrious leader learn and grow. At least that is my prayer.

Larry

Pete Responds

And, what galls me Larry, is Obama's ridicule of any opposition to his ideas. In essence it is the use of the Bully Pulpit to suppress ideas and free speech. And then there is the destructive Obamaism of distorted, manipulated words:

There is an evil art in being silent. Obama is an evil artist in words said, not said, but should have been said; and the deadly use of total silence.

Pete

Larry Answers Pete

Very informative and meaningful explanation, Pete. I agree. Obama seems to be extremely reluctant to take the lead in anything other than criticizing his critics. He is so small minded and childish. His small minded rants are no way for a leader to behave. Not only is he totally ineffective on the world stage (everyone sees him for the weak, petulant child he is) but he is actually dangerous. When the world is crying, nay, screaming, out for a strong leader to take charge and defeat Radical Islamic Terrorism, Obama slinks to the corner where he sits down and sucks his thumb with his back to the world.

A time in history that calls for strength and America has elected a milquetoast with no vision or understanding of what is swirling all around him and us. It is like millions of mosquitoes are all about him and he just occasionally swats one or two and then feels guilty for killing them. Tepid doesn't do justice to his foreign policy.

God help us all these next 13 months. I only pray we can survive the ineptest leader ever.

Larry

Pete Replies

Interesting points. Thanks Larry.

Obama's anger and repressed rage is so great that he has a massive reaction-formation against deaths, even necessary ones in a war. He seems fearful about little migrant children and their mothers on our Southern border. He often talks of his extreme negative reactions to visiting wounded warriors which he then uses to support his repugnance about "Boots -on-the-ground"---Even when he sends a few of them!

And regarding **migrants**, remember how he wouldn't even go down to see the little migrant kids on the Mexican border and refused to even view the Arizona border situation. Not that it matters much ultimately now, but I think Obama's vast blind-spot of denial (Denial is an unconscious process) stems from the facts of his early forced migrations. His mother's chaotic relationships with men led to his going to Indonesia, Hawaii and California as his mother fancied herself an anthropologist like Margaret Mead. Really at the core Obama was an abandoned child refugee psychologically. Trump may be wrong on where Obama's physical birth took place, but his psychological birth was as a floundering little migrant abandoned by his black father and his emotionally wandering white mother.

Unfortunately, he never had a good psychotherapy to help him move beyond his massive psychological blind spots.

Peter Olsson

Pete on Obama and His Illusions

I just listened to and observed Obama's chilly global-warming comments from Paris. Obama was at the height of his glory as global organizer to defeat global -warming, disease and genocide. Obama the delusional president of the world (Perhaps the universe) showed his true grandiose romanticized illusions. Through the power of his blaming, shaming, professorial pontifications he dismissed the ISIS attack in Paris as the terrible act of a small group of beasts with skills on the internet. He again instructed Putin and those horrible unfeeling Republicans as to the true course that history in Iraq, Syria and Europe will take. Our US billions spent to end the global carbon curse will serve as a good example as we mentor and massively support less fortunate countries in the world.

God help us for another year of this grandiose, mystical, relentlessly insecure man, and his approval-seeking dreams of glory!

Pete Olsson

Further Comments by Pete

I fear that Liberal Progressives (Really, Regressives), will have to experience larger numbers of Paris-like ISIS attacks in America like the recent Saudi Wahabi style attack in San Bernardino, California efore they wake up to the war America and The West is in with the Muslim Islamofascism of ISIS, Al Qaeda, Boko Haram, Turkish Islamists and the treacherous Shiite theocrats in Iran who Obama /Kerry have just given a clear path to nuclear weapons.

Islam itself must confront its radicals and reform themselves in order to enter the 21St century in their day-to-day applied theology. Muslims must become much more tolerant of contemporary Christianity (Not the Old Testament Judaism of pre-Jesus's love and grace).

Muslims need to be intolerant of their fanatical brothers and sisters---like the Muslim murderer couple who did the mass murder in California yesterday. That evil Muslim couple even left their 6 mos. old baby with friends while they went to do their murders.

Liberal Democrat Regressives need to wake up before it is too late. Sweetness and light, "Tolerance of diversity" and even Christian love have their limits when facing destructive radical Muslim Islamofascism. It is worth reading the Koran to understand Mohamadanism. I recommend starting in the latter chapters and not from start to finish.

Pete Olsson

And More

The more I think about it ---the greatest danger to America is Liberal American's irrational guilt about our prosperity, our Judeo-Christian heritage with its fostering of good character... and the fear of necessary war. (Our loss of the Vietnam war shook the foundation of our soul). Only a small percent of Americans have actually served in the military. Every dollar we spend on defense is worth it---including tactical nuclear devises.

Compared to the waste, fraud and spending abuse our congress refuses to cut, we need to increase our defense spending. We also need a revival of our American spiritual core. We are shocked by the dedication of youth to ISIS's radical Muslim jihad, but we don't let prayer in our schools. The mocking of God and prayer in liberal American media recently gives indication of our disorder of American character. Since when can prayer offend anyone? America dangerously separates church and state while Islam fuses church and state with feudal tribalism. Scary

Pete Olsson

Larry Answers Pete

Pete, you have hit the nail on the head totally. While we allow liberal Regressives to eviscerate our Judeo-Christian heritage and beliefs in every aspect of our culture, the Islamic fascists are killing in the name of their God, Allah. This is an extension of the centuries old Crusades which was a religious war. We are at war with a religion, albeit a morphed, kidnapped Islam, but a religious-zealot war nonetheless. They are not killing in the name of secular repressiveness.

I also think the San Bernardino massacre was an act of terror. Pure and simple. The question is whether it was an act of Radical Islamic Terror. And the answer is a resounding YES! They were Muslims. I think it may have been partly an act of workplace violence as they were obviously upset at one person at least and went on a killing spree at a Christmas party. I think their hatred for that one person sidetracked them from their other, original plans to execute an even larger, more deadly attack. I am certain there are more terrorists in this cell who will attack again in the future. Perhaps their main source of bombs and weaponry have been found and destroyed, which will keep them from committing an atrocity in the near future, but they are lying in wait and will begin accumulating more weaponry to be used on innocent victims. It is only a matter of time.

The war is real, and it has come to America. We are not safe, nor is ISIS contained as our gutless, witless non-leader pretends. His dangerous political correctness is going to result in many more American deaths. The blood will be on his hands. His lack of action, along with his premature withdrawal of troops from Iraq, led to the vacuum into which ISIS formed. And now his idiotic policies are leading to ISIS' growth, not their demise. More on this in an editorial I'll be sending out soon.

America has a lot to fear and too much of it is of our own feckless lack of leadership.

Larry

Rampage killers led secret life, hiding plans and weapons - LA Times

Actually, in my opinion, the Farook San Bernardino attack and surrounding circumstances convinced me from the beginning that it was an Al Qaeda style event. Farook and his wife had Saudi and Pakistani connections. (Pakistan has detested Obama since he took out Osama bin Laden in the way he did.)I think there were other Al Qaeda operatives involved, and the terror cell was planning other high media covered attacks in the LA area.

I keep using a simplistic analogy---If there was a movement to end pro baseball---Even avid NY Yankee fans and despised Boston Red Sox fans would band together to defend baseball. Even ISIS an intense competitor of Al Qaeda joins together about defeating Western Infidels in America, Europe and Israel. Though

I think Obama is an abject failure as a leader, his stubborn refusal to commit our troops on the ground to fight ISIS and Al

Qaeda is unfortunate. All the Islamofascist groups want to draw America into a ground war.

Local Arab tribal countries particularly Saudi Arabia need to use their vast wealth and their fighters to destroy ISIS. They also need to help shelter their Arab Syrian brothers and begin a massive effort to reform the destructive Wahhabism, they promote behind the scenes as they outwardly condemn them.

In WWII Hitler, Togo and Mussolini became fascist brothers.

Pete Olsson

Pete Writes to Larry

Larry

I have been giving a lot of thought to the process of vetting in general and for Muslim Jihadi's in particular: to investigate (someone) thoroughly to see if they should be approved or accepted for a job.

Definition--- to check (something or someone) carefully to make sure it is acceptable --or safe.

Years ago, I did many interviews of prospective psychiatry residency candidates and therapists at a low-fee psychotherapy clinic where I was clinical director. I. at the time, was concerned with the basic honesty, integrity and moral/ethical compass of those folks.

Things I learned:

1---The vetting interview process is daunting and difficult. (Hindsight trumps intuition.)

2---The receptionist and office staff often had valuable insight about applicants who were all smarminess at the interview with me?

3---A group interview of already established citizens (My senior resident students) were better at assessing the candidate than I.

So, my suggestion is to have already established Muslim American citizens (especially military and police) meet with prospective American citizens for in-depth interviews, specially to probe the sincerity, peacefulness and genuineness of the candidate's Mohamadanism.

Pete

Further Insights by Pete

Obama, the non-leading, non-governing, perpetual negative campaigner against

Republicans, hopes to change the hearts and minds of Muslim Islamo-fascists around the world by America's perpetual generosity and commitment against the evils of global warming that is the prime cause of terrorism.

I am sad to the core of my soul about what Obama's pathological narcissism has done to our country.

Pete Olsson

Larry Wrote In Response

There is so much wrong about this. Obama loves to spout off and brag about how wonderful and thorough his administration's vetting process is for all those thousands and thousands of refugees. Yet they could not discover one iota of evidence that the murderous California Islamic woman was a threat to America. So, immigration officials don't usually check social media posts? Really?

Everything I read tells me that is one of the Radical Islamic Terrorists primary recruiting tools. Gee, I would never think to look there.

But fear not, my friends. Obama is "reviewing" this program. Wow. I'm relieved. He isn't doing anything. Just "reviewing". What an insightful warrior. And Jeh Johnson says it is too soon to tell if the government missed signs of her radicalization. What galls me is the way these idiots toss around, so cavalierly, the use of generalized terms. They never admit that "they" did anything wrong or made a mistake. Nope. Not them. It was "the government" as if that is some distant, evil entity. Hells bells, Jeh.

The government is YOU!!!! YOU ARE THE GOVERNMENT!!!!

And, this incompetent and dangerous fool, is not prepared to say if there were any "red flags" that they should have seen. Good God, Jeh. If you can't keep us safe by seeing the obvious in only one person, how can Americans feel safe under your "watchful" eye? I suggest we cannot.

If this situation wasn't so serious it would be laughable. Alack and alas, it is not a joke other than to say the joke is on us for reelecting such a terrorist loving non-leader as our leader. Curses on every single voter who cast a ballot for this charlatan.

Larry

Further Facts to Support Larry's Thoughts

Tashfeen Malik, who along with her husband killed 14 people in Southern California reportedly passed three background checks by American officials before she moved from Pakistan to the United States and none of them found her social media posts about jihad.

An article in The New York Times

<http://www.nytimes.com/2015/12/13/us/san-bernardino-attacks-us-visa-process-tashfeen-maliks-remarks-on-social-media-about-jihad-were-missed.html?_r=0>

reports states that U.S. law enforcement officials discovered old and previously unreported postings as they investigated Malik and her husband Syed Rizwan Farook. Immigration officials don't usually check social media posts as part of their background checks, according to the newspaper.

Malik's path to the U.S. immediately highlighted the U.S. government's immigration vetting practices after she was identified as one of the attackers in San Bernardino, Calif. The Obama administration is reviewing the program, Homeland Security Secretary Jeh Johnson said Monday. He didn't specify what changes were going to be made.

Johnson said it was too soon to tell if the government missed signs that Malik may have been radicalized before she was approved for her visa. "That assumes, and this investigation is still under way, that there were red flags that were raised or should have been raised in the process of her admission to the United States, and I am not prepared to say that and I'm not prepared to make that declaration," Johnson said.

Pete Explores the use of the Overton Window Concept

OBAMA'S OVERTON WINDOW

Obama and Obamaites use of strawmen and predicate logic constantly have accumulated into a host of clichés we now call Political Correctness. This has formed a hope-and-changed view of America and what Obama falsely preaches as **our core values**. Obama in his brilliantly crafted and cadenced speeches he uses shaming, blaming and ridiculing as techniques of implementation.

The Overton Window is a political theory that describes as a narrow "window" the range of ideas the public will accept. According to this theory, an idea's political viability depends mainly on whether it falls within that window rather than on politicians' individual preferences.[1] It is named for its originator, Joseph P. Overton (1960-2003),[2] a former vice president of the Mackinac Center for Public Policy.[3] At any given moment, the "window" includes a range of policies considered politically acceptable in the current climate of public opinion, which a politician can recommend without being considered too extreme to gain or keep public office.

Overton described a spectrum from "freer" to "less free" with regard to government intervention oriented vertically on an axis. As the spectrum moves or expands, an idea at a given location may become more or less politically acceptable. His degrees or layers of acceptance of public ideas are roughly as follows in progression:

Unthinkable

Radical

Acceptable

Sensible

Popular

Policy

The Overton Window is an approach to identifying which ideas define the domain of acceptability within a democratic republic's possible governmental policies. Proponents of policies outside the window seek to persuade or educate the public in order to move and/or expand the window. Proponents of current policies, or similar ones, within the window seek to convince people that policies outside it should be deemed unacceptable. (Wikipedia)

Obama's constant repetition of HIS "Core value ideas" as if they are or have-to-be Americans' core values, are his clever way dictating what become his Overton -Window-based core values for America!

Pete and Larry Discuss a New Word – Microagression

The History of A Now Popular Word: **MICROAGGRESSION**

Microaggression refers to a comment or action that is subtly and often unintentionally hostile or demeaning to a member of a minority or marginalized group which has seen a decided increase in usage over the past several years, though the word is at least 45 years old. The first known written use of microaggression comes from January 1st of 1970, when the word appeared in the scholarly journal Universitas, in an article written by W. Hallermann (Reports on Crimes of Aggression).

Later that same year, microaggression began to be used by the man who is generally credited with having coined it, Dr. Chester M. Pierce, a professor of psychiatry at Harvard University. He wrote the following in *The Black Seventies*, a collection of essays: Pierce said, "Hence, the therapist is obliged to pose the idea that offensive mechanisms are usually a micro-aggression, as opposed to a gross, dramatic, obvious macro-aggression such as lynching."

For our edification...smile. Excluded are Obama's shaming, blaming, mocking and insulting of Republicans. I guess they would be termed macroaggressions of established truth by Obamaites.

Pete

Pete's Further Thoughts

Larry

The more I study an article by Kosner, the more I think he really has it nailed. Obama's narcissistic personality problems tend to entwine with his tepid, timid thought processes. He acts rigid, cocky and shaming of opponents because he vaguely senses critics are right. So, he must summon bravado to cover -over his relentless insecurity. The result is that his extreme caution about any aggressive military act is at the heart of it. His terror at being wrong pervades his identity and grandiosely wished-for legacy will be deeply devalued and pitied by historians. Literally, he has become aware that his emperor's new clothes don't keep you warm in winter.

Obama's caution may be correct even if he says so. That forms a paradox within a conundrum. A coward becomes king by default.

Pete

Larry Responds

For an American President to obscure his real strategy while distracting the citizenry with gauzy platitudes certainly has precedent. Franklin Delano Roosevelt talked out of the other side of his mouth for months as the Nazis and Japanese rampaged before Pearl Harbor and Hitler's declaration of war propelled the U.S. into World War II. Of course, FDR was determined to intervene, and Barack Obama seems just as determined to do the opposite vis-à-vis ISIS.

Perhaps Mr. Obama's confidence in his strategy of patience is well placed. From his own standpoint, it has the virtue of punting hard choices to his successor. Still, a major terrorist attack on the homeland or an escalating series of ISIS massacres at schools, shopping malls, sports events, or historic sites will convulse the country and discredit the President and his party in what is certain to be an inflamed election."

Sadly, the best defense is rarely the least offense.

Larry

Pete's Comment

I think Obama and his minions in their supreme grandiosity see Obama as the President of the World---not America. No surprises if we keep that perspective in view.

Pete

Pete Adds

It's all about Obama and Kerry's pathological Narcissism and not what's good for America. Iran is already firing missiles near the bow of our ships and China with its failing economy is showing signs, like Russia's Putin, of challenging us militarily big-time. The North Koreans will not forgo the opportunity to flex their nuclear muscles.

Obama in his pathological narcissistic bubble is merely trying to look too cool for school as he hides behind the Gun Control and Global Climate Change issues until his pathetic watch in the Whitehouse is over.

I think the next president should use Teddy Roosevelt and Reagan as a role-models and spend his or her first term undoing the Obama "Pen and Phone" fiascos while at the same time as he or she quietly builds up our military big-time. For example he/she could call for three more aircraft carriers and increase in military numbers and benefits to our sailors, airmen, marines and army stalwarts. I think our military, and particularly our tactical nuclear arsenal, needs to be built up so friendly turkey talk with Putin, Iran and China can successfully take place.

Good solid diplomacy requires strength behind words. That "Walk softly and carry big stick thing".

Pete

Pete Writes to Obama in Response to Chicago Violence

Dear Mr. Obama

Your tears and anger about American murders, while moving, is not enough. Please consider more vigorous enforcement of the existing gun laws. Urge Chicago's mayor to accept National Guard units if necessary to confiscate the illegal gang guns on the streets of Chicago. Double-down on your "Brother's Keeper Program". Use your Bully Pulpit to urge American fathers to stay with their families and if separated, to stay helpfully involved with their children. In addition, explore with congressional leaders the increased availability of mental health out-reach to, and engagement with, the untreated therefor more potentially violent mentally ill persons in America. It is unhelpful for you to shame, blame, guilt-provoke and mock congress about the gun murders in

America. It is your job to work WITH and join with congress toward solving the problem---not play the blame game.

Sincerely,

Peter Olsson MD

Larry Opines on Pete's Thoughts

If inanimate objects were responsible for crimes, cars would have been banned years ago. It is the operators of these mechanical devices who commit crimes. The method they choose to do so is relatively immaterial, until they escalate them to the realm of bombs. Unless and until a solid Conservative gets elected president, guns will continue to be blamed and the real issues will not get the focus they deserve.

Larry

Pete Comments on the Continuing Dream World by Obama and Kerry

In Obama and Kerry's utopian dream-world , they seem to think that by being civil, fair-minded, pseudo-friendly , pseudo-cooperative, in Obama's view A good example of good and decent behavior; that trust will build with Iran and they will become a make-nice "Partner" in peace with us like Russia. What absolute folly! What absolute misreading of human nature in general, and the Muslim and Arab world specifically. Strength, power and fair, firm verbal and if necessary decisive military confrontation leads to the possibility of grim respect from Iran, Russia, North Korea, Saudi Arabia, Assad's Syria, Libya, etc.

The one thing I agree with Obama about in his recent speech is that Congress should openly declare war on ISIS and all their metastatic malignant franchises. Then Obama should proceed to do what he must as POTUS but he is too weak and cowardly to do it all in the name of being a peace-maker.

Like Truman in Hiroshima, FDR in Dresden during WWII, a tactical nuke and certainly carpet-bombing or fire-bombing might be necessary because radical ISLAM and ISIS will not ever respond positively to American KOOM -Bye-YAH and "Being a Good Example to the world".

I once saw and heard Ralph Peters being interviewed on the book channel. The interviewer asked Peters what his religion was. Peters said---I long to be a Quaker. The interviewer asked--"Why aren't you? Peters said---"Because without non-pacifist warriors like me---no Quakers would exist in the world."

Pete

Larry Writes About Iran's Capture of our Navy Vessel

You could not be more correct Pete. For example, I cannot understand the fast capitulation of our Navy. They are trained warriors. The only answer that makes sense to me is that one boat had a problem and the other gave them cover. However, when the Iranians showed up, **Obama's Rules of Engagement** prevented them from fighting. This happens on the ground all the time, and now two naval threats are met with silence and an apology from a Navy Lieutenant, glowing praise from our daft Sec State Kerry and silence from our non-leader, Obama.

You are totally right Pete. Russia has belittled Obama, and now Iran, through their negotiators and their paltry Navy has embarrassed our military and China and N. Korea are watching. The South China Sea will be ruled by China and S. Korea better get ready because if Korea invades on Obama's watch we will retreat and run away.

Larry

Pete's Questions

I have several questions about John Kerry's impressive, diplomatic victory to free our captured sailors:

1---How could two patrol boats both have crippling engine failures? One maybe, two not possible.

2---Why would we not have support ships to aid the sailors when they floundered?

3---Why did our sailors not put up a fight if they were about to be captured?

4---Why would any apology ever be given by our sailors, Kerry or Obama? That is infuriating.

5---If we have a viable nuclear agreement with Iran with them getting billions soon, why would they even detain our sailors?

Could it be that the whole event was staged by Kerry/Obama and Iran to give a positive glow to the bogus Obama/Kerry capitulating agreement with Iran?

Interesting that Kerry was quick to extol the value of the 'deal' as why our sailors were freed.

My final question is who will be next to insult and test our Coward-in-chief? My guess is N Korea and, or, China. Putin has already benefitted from Obama's second term "New flexibility".

Obama is running for philosopher King of the world with UN help and probably a second worthless Nobel peace prize.

Pete Olsson

Larry Begins Discussion of Upcoming Election

With regards to Trump, you point out what you see as some of his strengths. I see it the same way. He will use one set of tactics to get elected, but once in the WH, for many reasons, he will govern wisely and surround himself with the best of the best. People who have actually done something. People who have led and made tough decisions. He will bring patriotism, courage, moral righteousness, military strength and strength of character to the position. I trust he will overturn much of Obama's deceitful and dangerous decisions. If Hillary has not already been indicted, I bet a Trump presidency (Christie as AG? Or Trey Gowdy?) would decimate her legally, as well she should be.

There have been many traitors to America in her history, but Benedict Arnold, Jane Fonda and Hillary Clinton are right at the top. I abhor all of them. Jane and Hillary should be in chains rotting away in Gitmo or some Federal Prison. Life terms with no chance of parole. Unfortunately, should a leftie Dem get elected president again, the first thing they would do is pardon Hanoi Jane and Benghazi Hillary.

Larry

Pete Writes

Larry

Many disagree with me, but I think Trump might think along these lines: Political correctness, leftwing media bias, an uninformed and irrational electorate and a vast herd of relentlessly dependent entitled masses inflicts America. Obama, through charisma, soaring utopian speeches, obfuscation and calculated lies, got elected. Obama, his Chicago machine and Obamaism seeks not to work with congress and Republicans, but to fragment and castrate the Republican Party. If a Republican is ever to get elected again, he or she must use paradoxical intention, bombastic bullying charisma and a reverse psychology on the electorate. (Trump uses Saul Alinsky principles in paradoxical and powerful ways).

Once he gets elected I think he would become similar to Ronald Reagan whose steady leadership, moral strength and excellent appointing of strong effective cabinet members and governing, military and diplomatic talent. Trump will also know how to say, "You're fired!"

Pete Olsson

Pete's Trump Imaginings

Larry, I imagine the following inner soliloquy of Donald Trump as he decided to run for president:

I observe America floundering. I see the economy sputtering after almost eight years of Obama's incompetent leadership, mushrooming regulations that hamstring job creation and ever

mushrooming national debt. I see bad trade deals with China, Mexico and other countries that hurt America. I see tax policies that drive jobs and industries out of America. I see increasing unemployment especially of young black Americans. I see law and order declining especially in big urban areas like Chicago Obama's home town. I see migrants and illegal immigrants given government assistance as American's go deeper into debt and poverty. Big expensive government programs favored by Democrat politicians are redundant and often failing. I see American military power, political leadership in the world decline to the extent that other nations laugh at us behind our backs as they give smarmy smiles to Obama. The Obama administration seems bound and determined to teach white America and Americans in general to be ashamed of their/our alleged hidden racism, bigotry, islamophobia, homophobia and xenophobia. He shames us and our political leaders who he paints as bad guys if they disagree with him. The constant search for micro-aggressions and political incorrectness by Obama-ites repulses me. I watched Obama and his minions insult, lie about, and distort the motives, intentions and character of sweet gentlemen like John McCain and Mitt Romney. I know I can be a strong, powerful and benevolent leader to rescue America. Obama uses his sneaky phone and pen to bring America down a peg or two and share it's /our wealth around in some neo-socialist ways. I know and have participates in the rigged American political system that is floundering. I know where the crooked bodies are buried. I made billions legally through the flawed system in America. I will be a benevolent Trojan Horse to lead a hopefully bloodless revolution in America. I will use a P.T. Barnum, applied reality TV model of politics to win. I can't be bought by anyone. America will be great and safe again. I love America so much that I will make mistakes and try to honestly correct them. I will listen to as many Americans as I can. I will talk straight to them about what I see as the truth of where America must go to be great and safe again.

More of Pete's Thoughts

We can call Obama names and mock him (As HE does to Fox and Republicans),but, Hillary will certainly extend his Democrat Socialism. I think that is why Sanders has competed well with Hillary. Obamaism has already transformed much of America irrevocably. Rubio needs to repeat his point over and over again. It goes way beyond some narrow debate tricks. Rubio's point must be made urgently and repeatedly. Repetition is the life-blood of learning and mastery. I think Rubio was making up in small part for how neglected his point about Obama and Obamaism has been among all the candidates. Obama has NOT been incompetent, stupid, etc. He has transformed America into a dependency- mired, central government state. Obama recently met with Sanders and I think they talked about Bernie's role in extending Obama's democrat socialism and even further into a fantasied world-wide utopia of neo-Marxism disguised as Obama's version of Democracy and "social justice". Obama slyly calls this, "Our American Values".

Pete

Larry Answers Pete

You're so right, Pete. The left bases most of their decisions on emotions. They never use their head or cogent thinking to decipher and solve any problem. Costs? Never considered. Whether the costs are economic, social, personal, or spiritual. They just forge ahead with destructive policies and thoughts that, at first blush and only on the surface, sound nice. But they never dig below the surface. Like free college for all. How much will that cost and who will pay?

Never considered. And before we flood the streets with educated, but lacking-in-the-ability-to-think individuals, lets create some real jobs so these graduates can actually earn a living someday. McDonalds has enough educated imbeciles.

Sad is a most appropriate term to define today's America. And, I agree that the time may be too late. Far, far too many Americans now have tasted the free stuff of the left. Either they will not elect a conservative, (and I suspect there are not enough of us left to do it) or they will throw a conservative out of office at the first opportunity after he/she insists on policies that actually make people work and get properly educated.

Rubio is right. Obama knows exactly what he is doing, and he succeeded in fundamentally transforming America into a third world country. From now on it is everyone for themselves, except for the masses lining up for every imaginable freebie. America's demise is simply now a matter of time.

Larry

Pete's Response

In addition to the Free Stuff horde, there are a vast herd of idealizing liberal progressive worshipping people that seem to merge with and fuse with leaders like Obama, Sanders and Hillary. They have a Romanized and "Feel Good" emotion-laden state. They feel they are loving do-gooders and are glad for the evil rich to pay for all the tender loving care of the less fortunate. They are the feel good benevolent antiwar Americans. (Really isolationists who have forgotten or don't care about 9/11). They don't apply history, they think they are making it beautiful and entertaining. Sad, sad

Pete

Pete Writes to Obama

Mr. Obama:

I ask respectfully that you stop saying "That is not US", when you speak out about a national or international issue involving America. My friends, family, colleagues, others and I know who we are, what our core values and morals are without you telling us or the world what they are... or in your opinion, should be.

I also ask that you stop your arrogant, shaming, blaming, insulting and guilt-provoking tone when addressing US or our congressional representatives. Disagreement with your presidential dictates and divisive postures does not mean we are racist, lacking in compassion or empathy. You have failed in your ability to work with our elected representatives so you best examine your own core values and responsibilities as president.

Sincerely yours,

Peter Olsson MD

Thank you for writing. While we may not see eye-to-eye on every issue, I want you to know I'm listening.

In a country as big and diverse as ours, there are bound to be disagreements. Our democracy has embraced this truth since its founding, when the power to shape our government and our shared future was distributed among the American people. Your voice matters, and our Nation's progress has always depended on people like you who act on the obligation to speak out on issues that are important to them.

During the remainder of my term, I'll keep striving to make sure our politics reflect the goodness and decency of the American people. Because beyond our differences, we are one people, and we rise and fall together.

Thank you, again, for writing.

Sincerely,

Barack Obama

Pete's Angry Response to New Identity Politics by Obamaites

In its bizarre fashion the Obamaites blur together transsexualism, fetishistic cross-dressers, transvestites, pre-adolescents /adolescents in identity crises and sexually ambivalent borderline psychotic personality disorders as if they were normal lifestyle choices. All this in defiance or denial of medical, psychiatric and psychological research.

Pete

Pete's and Larry's Tongue-in-Cheek Conclusions on Obama

THE OBAMA LEGACIES

1---Free Dope and Related Pot Brain Damage (Obama, in a speech comments that pot is no more damaging than alcohol.)

2---Subtle disregard of traditional American values and morals.

3---Military Weakness of Dangerous Proportions

4---Promotion of Rampant Economy Dependency

5---Faux championing of the middle class while damaging it.

6---Decline in Quality of Medical Care, especially the poor. (Obamacare)

7---Increase in Costs of Medical Care (Obamacare)

8---Promoting Racial Division and Hate (Black Lives NOT All Lives Matter)

9---Disrespect for Police Authority (Cambridge Police and Prof Gates, Ferguson Incident)

10---Political Prevarication and Obfuscation (Pseudo-transparency)

11---Decline of the Coal and Petroleum Industries

12---Promotion of Illegal Immigrant Invasions (Catch and Release and release and...)

13---Foolish and Dangerous Nuclear Deal with Iran.

14---Damaging Israel with shallow praise and neglect. (Hatred of Prime Minister Netanyahu)

15---Cowardice and timidity in Iraq and Afghanistan (Deadly Rules of Engagement)

16---Leaving America in a mess for the next POTUS.

Pete's Thoughts

As I have been saying since August 2008---Obama's narcissism is the core of his unconscious-based rage at traditional America. Our unconscious is a powerful motivational force. Dinesh D'Souza wrote about *OBAMA'S AMERICA* and early in 2009 with his book, *THE ROOTS OF OBAMA's RAGE* and D'Souza's career was almost destroyed by Obama's injustice department.

Marco Rubio was so on-target during the debate when he said, "Obama knows exactly what he is doing to America".(Marco was harshly criticized for repeating this thesis over and over.)

In essence, Obama has fiddled with America's soul as America smolders in free dope, spurious change and spiritual mange.

Pete Olsson

Pete Derides Obamaists Campaign Defenses of His Legacy and Hillary's Continuation of it

Pete's Rant

Congress needs to subpoena Ben Rhodes the assistant national "Insecurity" advisor. He in the tone of his narcissist boss had the flagrant arrogance to brag to the NY Times that he/they were able to deceive and bamboozle the "Stupid" media and the public about key issues around the bad nuclear deal with Iran. With the resignation of the head of the Joint Chiefs of Staff, I no longer trust anyone in the abysmal Obama administration to give any truthful info to US.

I particularly am disgusted with Kerry, Susan Rice and the state department spokespersons or the presidential press secretary. Sad state of public affairs indeed. I am disgusted with the Obama administration's deceptions about Iran's despicable treatment of our sailors and Kerry's disgusting obfuscating comments and apologizing.

All presidential spokespersons are under pressure, and Tony Snow and Dana Perino set high standards, but, I do not know how any spokesperson for president Obama can sleep at night or live with themselves.

By the way, has anyone heard hide or hair about Netanyahu or Israel? I think our State-Controlled- Media (ObamaVESTIA) is getting flagrant, not through the usual political spinners, but by deliberate lies and manipulations.

Woodward tries, Bernstein's integrity is shot to hell. As Simon and Garfunkel sang "Where are you Joe DiMaggio when our nation's heart turns to you?" Billy Graham is too frail. Rubio got bushwhacked. Can Trump's ego be channeled; his relentless ad homonym crudeness's be atoned-for?

I for one do not see Trump's Narcissism as pathological, It only appeared that way because it takes gargantuan strength of a strong ego to win against the scourge of new forms of neo-Marxism and Democrat party socialism run amuck in America.

Pete Olsson

Pete Raves

Yesterday impulsive Obama made insulting, ignorant and inappropriate comments about Trump while on his Asian apology tour. He said world leaders are wary and worried about Trump. He gave no examples nor did any 'world leaders' speak for themselves about Trump. Obama was illustrating the Dunning-Kruger Effect. I think it is good if "World Leaders" are wary and worried about Trump or any president or presidential candidate. World politics, military deployment and diplomacy and decision-making is not a polite cocktail party, buddy-buddy or mutual admiration society for leaders.

I believe Obama is so endlessly insecure, indecisive and weak that he has no business insulting Trump in the world media. Me thinks Obama PROJECTITH too much.

Pete Olsson

Pete Speaks to Larry

Larry

You touch on what I think is one of Obama's domains of incompetence and destructiveness to America namely HIS totally politically driven and foolish appointments!

Bumbling spokespersons, Smug Ben Rhoades, Brain damaged Biden. Crooked Hillary, Egotistical, Medal Throwing, Pretend Hero John Kerry. Arrogant Holder at AG (And we will see if Lynch has guts soon), Susan the liar Rice, Jeh the political hack Johnson at Homeland Insecurity and somewhat reasonable, but weak Ash Carter at defense (Hagel and Gates at least finally spoke out after leaving). The incompetent EPA chief, The incompetent chiefs of the VA, The smidgen star at the IRS, Lois Lerner and Sibelius at care-less Obamacare. Thank God Obama is being foiled so far regarding the Supreme Court. At least Obama's economic team members fled the leaky ship with various excuses. Geithner, the guy who couldn't handle his own Turbo-Tax finances. (Jack Lew seems much better but still yes-Manish). Idiotically leftist Napolitano and all the other Obamaites underlings.

Think about and compare: Roberto Gonzales's integrity, Rumsfeld's integrity and genius, Colin Powell and Condi Rice, Gates, Paulson (Not so much), Dick Cheney a true man of integrity, Chertoff and Tom Ridge.

Pete Olsson

Larry adds his Ire

Pete, your list of both the good, bad and ugly is superb. Sometimes there are so many bad and ugly that I forget all their names, but you put them all in proper perspective. Trump can't hold a candle to your nicknames...smile. But their crimes, lies, obfuscations and deliberate attacks on America are all food for the lawyers in the new AG office should Trump prevail. His first four years in office may very well be dutifully spent in pursuing criminal and treasonous charges against all of these traitors.

Washington, DC and, especially this administration, is corrupt from the top down. It is always the case. Leaders set the example for their organizations. They establish the culture. In his rush to dismantle the most productive and wonderful country ever devised on this earth he has lost his way and his soul. Now we need a true patriot to rebuild what Obama has torn down. I sense a revolution of large perspective.

Larry

Larry Opines Further

Arising from a recent discussion between us and friends about the core of education in America, emerged this excellent brief essay by Larry Messner:

Schools should be primarily places of education and academics. But implicit in getting a good education is the spiritual side. I don't want a school to be advocating any one religion over another, but acknowledging spirituality is part of a person's overall growth. To pretend spirituality is not a part of an overall, well rounded person is to deny humanity. We expect our schools to turn out caring, empathetic individuals as well as students who actually know something useful. What good is being a doctor, lawyer, auto mechanic, business leader or any other vocation if we haven't infused in our children some ethics and morality?

When I teach my leadership course, I stress ethics, morality and honesty. I have witnessed far too many leaders who have a serious moral deprivation and I developed and wrote my course in the time frame of Bernie Madoff and others. And, to me, part of being an effective leader is reliance on their ethics which is born out of spirituality. I believe teaching spirituality, morals, ethics, honesty and philosophy to be a vital part of a good education. It is the removal of any and all religious beliefs (you needn't teach a specific religion in order to teach essential and valuable Christian/Judeo principles upon which this country was founded) that I find so lacking in today's academic institutions at all levels. When we deny the teaching of any spirituality we are advocating a secular/progressive approach which violates my belief system just as much as my beliefs often offends them.

I advocate a well- rounded approach to education, not a restrictive one. I want no "safe spaces" in my course, teachings or campus. Diversity is a well sought-after ideal on campuses but fails unless it includes diversity of thought which, in my estimation, is the most important aspect of diversity.

Larry

Larry Comments Further on Education in America

I believe that when we get too far in either direction we are headed astray. Whether it be the KKK (actually a Democrat development) or the Black Lives Matter mob, they fail to see any other viewpoint other than their own narrow and perverted one. True education and growth comes from listening to and debating viewpoints in contrast to one's own. Safe spaces have no place on any campus for any reason. If you cannot discuss and defend your beliefs, then maybe they aren't so ingrained in you and you may want to readdress your reasons for holding them.

We grow when we are challenged. Sometimes we learn more from confrontation than we do from blind following. I have never found the act of avoidance to be constructive. How "safe spaces" ever became acceptable on campuses is beyond me. I have always believed academia should be the place where free thought and discussion of those thoughts are fully and openly discussed.

Socrates is rolling over in his grave....

Larry

Author's Combined Thoughts

Both authors agree that our American education system's problems began long before Obama's administration. But, the situation has worsened since he and his minions have advocated massive projects of political incorrectness -laced policies, leftist propaganda, and shame-based speechifying. Many American university students seem to passively accept the idea that liberal progressive political thinking and values are the "The correct way to think", morally, spiritually, ethically and legally. In their eyes, Conservative thinking and philosophy is cold, lacing in empathy, even cruel and uncaring.

Pete and Larry

Pete Observes

This AM Mitch McConnell was interviewed on fox news. He confirmed my observations about Obama's pathological narcissism. The head of the Senate said that there was literally no two-way conversations with Obama. McConnell said Obama always incessantly, relentlessly had to prove he was the smartest guy in the room. The only time there was some fruitful work was when Obama brought Biden along. Biden listened and discussed compromises. Obama didn't.

In my opinion, Obama's pathological narcissism impaired his ability to have genuine dialogue with Congress. He then shames and accuses congress of not working with him. It is Obama's job to work with congress not insult them. Most all politicians have plenty of normal narcissism but in dysfunctional presidents like Obama, malignant narcissism prevents their effective work. I think once Trump is elected his apparent thin skin of narcissism and overconfidence will not get in the way of governing or working with Congress, our enemies, and our allies. The Art of the Deal comes to Washington as Trump would say, "Big Time".

Pete

A Headline that Prompted Pete's Further Thoughts

'Iran Lied': Israel PM Netanyahu Presents 'Conclusive Proof' of Iran's 'Secret Nuclear Weapons Program' | Mediaite Cable

Pete Writes to Larry Regarding Headline

Larry

As I said from the moment I read the provisions of the ill-advised Obama-Kerry non-treaty treaty, (which was never ratified by the Senate and opposed by the Senate Leader, Schumer), it was and still is clear that it was pure folly to trust Iran to inspect itself and to approve of spot, unannounced inspections.

And billions in cash to Iran arriving under cover of darkness on a private plane to sweeten the deal. Naive or foolish Obama claimed that we owed Iran the billions in interest on the money of theirs we froze during sanctions. He said we saved money by paying them the interest promptly because we would lose the appeals in the world court. Bologna. They owed us for our hostages they held and tortured. Obama be damned.

And, Obama still continues to lecture Americans that our values should be as he declares them to be.

Angrily Pete Writes to Obama

Dear President Obama

I grew up in Brooklyn and Long Island, New York. I studied medicine and practiced it in Houston Texas for thirty years and in New Hampshire for twenty- five years. I am not, nor ever have been a racist. When you got elected our president I had high hopes for your success. Before your first term was over I concluded two things. One, I totally disagreed with your policies and approach to governing. Two, I grew to dislike your blaming of everyone else for your abject failures as a leader. The persistence of this trait led me to dislike and distrust you, your judgement and leadership. To thoroughly dislike and distrust you are not racist beliefs. As a psychiatrist, I think you need to consider your own soul to explore your unconscious reverse racism. For various reasons, I think you dislike or feel unconscious conflict about the white half of your racial heritage.

Sincerely yours,

Peter Olsson

Larry Responds

Pete. Spot on...I love it. It is so to the point. I agree completely. Obama is a born-again racist. He learned it at the feet of his mentor, Rev Wright. To look America in the eye and say he never heard any racism spew from the wrong Wright is an obvious lie bordering on covering up racism. As a student of leadership, I can unequivocally say Obama is a total failure as a leader. Every book on leadership I have ever read, and I have many in my own personal library including many biographies and autobiographies about some of our greatest leaders, all say that leaders take the blame for ALL failures on their watch. Period! As everyone knows, Obama has never accepted the blame for anything. And now, he is out blaming again. He just can't seem to help himself.

Larry

A Final Poem on Obama by Peter Olsson

Political Charisma Run Amok: Chameleon Obama's Capoeira

The charismatic obfuscator-in-chief, trots on stage.

Cockily strutting to the lectern, his chin juts skyward.

The teleprompter guides words crafted so officiously.

A charming smarmy grin is his wordless preamble.

His purported empathy defines pure political power.

The baritone voice tries to claim America's heartbeat.

Borrowed intonation resembles Martin, Billy and John.

He foists faux nobility upon scared collective souls.

"Hope and Change" are mantras finding false forms,

They have now become "Dope and Spiritual Mange."

Acorns and green science pose socialistic disguises.

The emperor and czars have dazzling dress clothes.

Ingenious artist at strawman crafting and creating.

His utopian words are intoxicants sheep can embrace.

He is so defensive when his judgment is questioned.

Obama would best be mindful of Eden's shadow side.

America tantalized by his thirty pieces of silver debt.

An inevitable urge and danger, for Jesus to find Judas.

Sadly, Barack Jr. confuses cogent critics with enemies.

He takes global trips to apologize for our prosperity.

Subconsciously loathing Wall Street's "fat cats", to be

Destroyed for savaging dreams from his father;

A Barack who hated colonial capitalism with a fury,

He cheated and lied...as he drank himself to death.

To honor his dad, Barack Jr. feels he must be godlike.

A mesmerizing messiah, selling socialist salvation.

A snake oil balm his redistribution of U.S wealth.

Finally citing omniscient criteria for Hellfire deaths.

To protect US war-weary souls from the terror beasts.
Only a God uses drones for sacred forms of killing;
while denying that such action expands Al Qaeda.
Barack and Hillary soaked in Benghazi Blood-gate.
Let us all hail to the arrogant prevaricator-in-chief.
And his smart fellow Alinsky-loving heiress apparent,
who wonders why spilled Benghazi Blood still matters.

Review Requested:
If you liked this book, would you please provide a review at
Amazon.com?
Thank You

www.ingramcontent.com/pod-product-compliance
Lightning Source LLC
Chambersburg PA
CBHW051453250726
48655CB00001B/387